What people are saying about Blessings From A Thousand Generations:

"If you wish to solve the mystery of your family heritage, mend the negative love bonds that have plagued your life, and reconnect with your divine nature, this book is a 'must read' for you!"

-Robert A. Giacalone, Ph.D., Temple University

Combining ancient wisdom, personal experiences, innovative concepts and practical exercises, *Blessings from a Thousand Generations* will help countless people heal old wounds and accelerate their personal development. Donna Evans Strauss has masterfully integrated a variety of groundbreaking ideas and written an indispensable guide for those seeking to better understand themselves.

David Schwerin, Ph.D., Author of *Conscious Capitalism and Conscious Globalism*

We live in a time when many families are in need of healing and individuals are seeking meaning in life. In *Blessings from a Thousand Generations*, Donna Evans Strauss provides an excellent, practical and holistic tool to help families and individuals heal their negative love bonds and receive the blessings of their ancestors.

Rev. Tom Abugelis

BLESSINGS

FROM A

THOUSAND
GENERATIONS

WHAT OUR BIBLICAL ANCESTORS CAN TEACH US
ABOUT HEALING OUR FAMILIES TODAY

Donna Evans Strauss

BALBOA.
PRESS

A DIVISION OF HAY HOUSE

Balboa Press books may be ordered through booksellers or by contacting:

Balboa Press
A Division of Hay House
1663 Liberty Drive
Bloomington, IN 47403
www.balboapress.com
1-(877) 407-4847

Because of the dynamic nature of the Internet, any Web addresses or links contained in this book may have changed since publication and may no longer be valid. The views expressed in this work are solely those of the author and do not necessarily reflect the views of the publisher, and the publisher hereby disclaims any responsibility for them.

Unless otherwise noted, scripture is taken from the HOLY BIBLE, NEW INTERNATIONAL VERSION®. Copyright © 1973, 1978, 1984 Biblica. Used by permission of Zondervan. All rights reserved.

The author of this book does not dispense medical advice or prescribe the use of any technique as a form of treatment for physical, emotional, or medical problems without the advice of a physician, either directly or indirectly. The intent of the author is only to offer information of a general nature to help you in your quest for emotional and spiritual well-being. In the event you use any of the information in this book for yourself, which is your constitutional right, the author and the publisher assume no responsibility for your actions.

Any people depicted in stock imagery provided by Thinkstock are models, and such images are being used for illustrative purposes only.
Certain stock imagery © Thinkstock.

ISBN: 978-1-4525-3192-2 (sc)
ISBN: 978-1-4525-3193-9 (e)

Library of Congress Control Number: 2010919431

Printed in the United States of America

Balboa Press rev. date: 02/14/2011

In memory
of my father,
Peter Sergeant Clark Sr.

Our death is not an end if we can live on in our children and the younger generation. For they are us; our bodies are only wilted leaves on The Tree of Life –Albert Einstein

Contents

ACKNOWLEDGMENTS

SPECIAL ACKNOWLEDGMENTS

I want to thank Michele Bourgeois, my good friend, colleague, and co-founder of the Living From Grace Program in Canada. Without her love, joyful support, and expertise, this book and the program wouldn't have had a platform to manifest.

I want to thank Dr. Barbara Ann Brennan, my teacher and mentor for eighteen years.

I want to thank Eva Pierrakos for her 257 Pathwork Lectures that are at the cutting edge of Transpersonal Psychology and transformed my life.

I want to thank my Pathwork Helpers and teachers, Carolyn Tilove and Susan Thesenga. Both have inspired my life and work in profound ways.

I want to thank Sophfronia Scott for the hours of editing and coaching we spent together to bring *Blessings from a Thousand Generations* to publication.

I want to thank Heather Kabat for her ability to listen and transform my ideas into the illustrations presented in this book.

I want to thank Sara Pierce for her care and editing services when this book was only an idea.

FOREWORD

This is a day of great celebration, seeing the first of Donna's books ready to go out into the world. I met Donna Evans Strauss five years ago. After two days in her Healing Addictions (Trust) workshop, I remembered the Bible passage when someone asked Jesus what the kingdom of heaven is like. He said it's like finding a great treasure buried in a field. You immediately go and sell everything you have to buy that field and what it holds. Donna was inviting each of us to find that treasure—buried inside. As she honored the treasure she saw there, she called on us to seek and find that great treasure in our family members and all other people as well.

The breadth and depth of Donna's work leaves me in awe and deeply moved. Watching how she embodies her teaching has kept me coming back for more, even when I was afraid to look into the parts of my life that needed awareness and healing. But doing so has given me the joy and peace of sensing the Great, Holy Spirit moving in and through all our lives. As the oldest child in a minister's family, I'd heard and longed to know more about grace as I was growing up. But I left the Christian church with a broken heart in 1979 and, after 27 years, had given up on finding any way back. A little over a year ago, after this work made it possible to receive many gifts of grace and healing, I returned to my local church family with an open heart.

Like a bridge, Donna's healing vision encompasses those who participate in a church, synagogue, or other faith community and those who seek spiritual guidance elsewhere. It has grown from her work in energy healing with Barbara Brennan, her Pathwork Helpership training, and her private practice as a spiritual healer and counselor. Her passion for healing has also led her to teach conscious parenting skills and to work with addictions.

Over the last five years, Donna has worked like a whirlwind to open, stretch, and articulate her vision and work. Those of us who have taken her courses, here and there throughout the U.S. and in Canada, have been honored to witness her work emerge and integrate from one class to the next. I expect it will continue to expand and deepen. This book and the other ones she's been writing make it possible now to reach many others who are hungry for spiritual nourishment, who long to find a way through despair or loss of meaning in their lives. In the coming time, as we shift our very understanding of life on this planet and our place in the universe, I believe this book will give vital comfort, hope, and direction to many.

I've read and contemplated the ideas presented in this book many times, both as a student of the Living from Grace Program and as an editor. These words don't stay on the page; they've taken root in me and rise up in new situations every day. They give me another perspective and remind me to trust the God-Realization process—knowing that with God, anything is possible. Even trying out one little step at a time has unfolded deep healing, transformation, and potential in all my relationships: with my Source, my family, work, and the larger community. So I encourage you to let the words of this book soak into your heart and mind, over and over, and see what happens. Those same-old situations, relationships, and problems in your life may begin to take on new meaning and possibility, just waiting for you to realize what is needed to transform them.

I also recommend using *Blessings from a Thousand Generations,* which outlines the God-Realization Process, with Donna's next book, *Restoring Our Divine Nature: The I AM Meditation Workbook*. Saying the *I AM* Meditation will help you to experience and integrate all the wisdom and healing potential that *Blessings* offers.

For Donna and all she has done with the life and relationships she was born into, for all of Donna's teachers along the way, starting with her father, and for this book and the others soon to follow, I give thanks.

May you find heaven within, just waiting for you to remember...

Susan Beach
Edmonton, Alberta
November 23, 2010

INTRODUCTION

If you don't know [your family's] history, then you don't know anything. You are a leaf that doesn't know it is part of a tree. ~Michael Crichton

Imagine for a moment being born into a family where the only person you know is your father. All the branches of the family tree are cut off. Your mother, grandparents, aunts, uncles, and cousins are nowhere to be found, never to be discussed. Then, to add to the confusion, you later discover that the man you presumed to be your father may not be your biological father. This was my experience! My Family Tree of Knowledge was void of any relatives; I had only the man I had assumed was my dad. You might be thinking, "What happened? How is that possible?" Or maybe, "Wow! That is one dysfunctional family!" I know I did! But then I discovered an important truth: God seeks us out regardless of the dire situations or crooked paths we are born into. The spiritual journey of my family would unravel a greater mystery. In time, I learned this journey went beyond my family. In all families, the Tree of Knowledge is the key that leads us back to the Garden of Eden and oneness with God. This book is about *God Realization* and the spiritual journey of the family. It is a guide to attaining healing, wholeness, and holiness, regardless of our life path or of any situation we find ourselves born into.

Many of us have adopted the term *dysfunctional family* to describe what I now call *positive and negative love bonds*. For those of us who were born into the sins of our parents and ancestors, our journey will be to unravel this mystery, find our true selves, and release the negative love bonds that hold us hostage to the past. We can become free from the old, archaic beliefs and wounds of our Family Tree of Knowledge. Like Moses journeying to the top of Mount Sinai to contemplate his Jewish roots and free his people from the bondage, we will need to listen to God, uncover our roots, reclaim our true heritage, and find our own Promised Land.

Moses did exactly that. The Pharaoh's sister adopted him, and he was raised in the home of a king with the finest of education, clothes, and food at his disposal. Yet within him was the wisdom of his heritage, the knowledge of his Jewish roots. This knowledge catapulted Moses on a spiritual journey to reclaim his heritage and to free and restore his people by leading them back into right relationship with God.

I believe we have a lot to learn from Moses, not only from his place in history as God's anointed teacher, but also from his spiritual journey. The Ten Commandments are Spiritual Keys to awakening our right relationship with God. In fact, there are many stories in the Old and New Testaments that lead us into right relationship with the light within us. In this book, I explore many of these stories and how they can lead you to God Realization.

Religious Experience

You might be thinking, "I already know these stories and use them in my daily life." Others of you may think, "Those stories are old and have nothing to do with me." You may say, "I gave up on the church and God long ago." Yet, exploring our roots, our images about God, and uncovering this deeper wisdom can change our lives in wonderful ways.

My early religious life was limited to only a few experiences. My first memories were of attending a Baptist church in Lawrence, Indiana. I remember this church so vividly because of a situation with my father. I was around five years old at the time and had been sent to my room for doing something wrong, as Dad sent us there to think about our behavior on occasion. I crawled up on the top bunk where I slept and waited for my dad to come talk with me. I remember him standing by the bed and asking, "Well, Donna, did you think about what you did?"

I said, "Yes, Daddy. I don't know why you are punishing me. It is not fair."

"What?" he asked. "You need to think about your behavior."

I said, "I did, Daddy. It is not fair, Daddy. Somebody better go out and get that devil and punish him. Can you get the devil, Daddy? It is not my fault. Somebody has to get that devil and make him go away."

My dad was shocked and asked, "Who told you that?"

"I learned it at church, Daddy. They say the devil is the one who makes us do bad things. Daddy, please make him go away."

After that, we started to attend a Methodist church nearby. When I was in the seventh grade, we moved to the country. We never attended church after that move, and it wouldn't be until years later that God would seek me out.

You may have a similar story—a childhood version of God based on your religious experiences, parents, and teachers. Everyone forms beliefs about God based upon their childhood memories. We adapt to the beliefs of our parents and the society in which we live. Some of these stories can be rich and fulfilling, while others leave us with a sense of emptiness. In the latter, we become lost sheep trying to find our way home. This is what happened to me.

My life was busy in the early teen years and into high school. I graduated the summer before my senior year and started working at RCA Records and Tapes in Indianapolis. Like many of our youth today, I wasn't connected to church or any other spiritual practices. I was a rebel, strong, and wanted to do life my way. As far as I was concerned, I didn't need anyone, least of all God. My life experiences had taught me that relatives and God were non-existent. I learned from my father's example that I could do things on my own without anyone. But, oh boy, was I wrong!

Miracles on My Path

Over the course of the next several years, I found little miracles dropped in my path, and these eventually led me to God. The first occurred when I was twenty. I landed a position as a counselor at the Madison County Juvenile Center. One evening at work, I had a spiritual experience that changed my life forever. It happened immediately after a thirteen-year-old girl attempted suicide by scratching her wrist with glass from a broken light bulb. I was sitting in the office writing up an incident report about this case when I noticed, for the first time, copies of the Bible sitting on the bookshelf. In my desperation and sense of helplessness, I picked one up and started to pray for the children. I told God, "I am only a child myself. How can I help your children?" Within minutes of me opening the Bible, Pastor Fields arrived at the door and asked if he could help the children. When help showed up just when I asked for it, my life was changed, and I was opened up to the power of prayer.

Later, the prayers of Pastor Fields assisted me in finding my mother, after being estranged from her for nineteen years. I moved to New Jersey to get to know her, but this unfortunately threw me into the path of my mother's mental illness without the tools to deal with it or an understanding of how to handle it. During this struggle, I was blessed with the guidance of two wonderful people, Hesh and Babs, who helped me get back on my feet. I rented the upstairs of Hesh's home, and Hesh and Babs became my surrogate parents. God works in our life in this way, by placing people in our path to help guide us on our journey. Each one is a great teacher, and many act as angels.

At the time, I was dating a man named George, and even his brief presence in my life seemed to be for a reason. Unbeknownst to me, George came from the neighborhood where my father was raised. One day my dad was describing the cemetery where his own father was buried, giving particular details about the hilltop view near the grave. He couldn't remember where the place was, but he was curious to know if his mother had been buried there as well, and he asked George to take me there to investigate. As we drove, George realized my dad's description seemed strangely familiar; in fact, it sounded just like the place where his own mother was buried. I was confused at first when he showed me her plot, but then he pointed out things from my dad's description and said he was pretty sure my grandparents might be in the vicinity too. Sure enough, they were just five graves away! We found the coincidence surreal and exciting—not to mention just a little bit spooky. George eventually moved to California and our relationship ended, but I've often wondered if he was placed in my life solely for the purpose of leading me to my grandparents—a crucial piece in my search for my family heritage.

Soon after, I met and married my husband, Jeff Strauss, and adopted his son Matthew. Since I wasn't attached to my Christian roots and Jeff was already raising Matthew in the Jewish tradition, I joined them. We attended synagogue on holidays and guided our sons, Matt and Brandon, through Hebrew school. But still, I felt detached from my roots, and it wouldn't be until twenty-seven years later that I would discover how these two great religions, Christianity and Judaism, are tied together. It was this discovery that would become the inspiration for this book.

Because of my prayer experience with Pastor Fields, I was deeply interested in healing and how prayer works. I studied meditation and other healing modalities and eventually entered the Mental Technology Program at Hahnemann University in Philadelphia to study psychology. My longing to understand hands-on healing grew. I remember saying to God one night, "I want to attend the best healing school to learn about healing and what is happening in my life." Later that month, I was visiting *Henry's Rock and Gem* store when a man in a wheelchair came in. I remember thinking, "Oh God, I wonder if he could get up and walk? If Christ could heal the lame and sick, could this man walk again?" In the same moment, my superego said, "Oh, please, Donna, don't talk to this man. You are out of your mind." So, I decided to mind my own business and go away.

Later that evening, I went to my class at the library, and guess what! This man in the wheelchair, Tad, rolled into the classroom. We began to talk about healing, and he gave me a book titled *Hands of Light: A Guide to Healing Through The Human Energy Field,* by Barbara Ann Brennan. Tad said he had seen her for healings.

I thought, "Is this an answer to my prayer?" I was excited about the book. My husband encouraged me to find out if the author was teaching any programs. In April of 1987, as a birthday gift to myself, I attended her Introductions Workshop and decided to enter her program, as well as continuing my studies at Hahnemann. After graduating from both programs in 1992, I began teaching at the Barbara Brennan School. I wanted to create a bridge between psychology and what I was experiencing at the Brennan School. The hands-on-healing work seemed to be at the cutting edge of consciousness studies.

Barbara Ann Brennan, PhD, is a pioneer and leader in the field of Healing Science and Transpersonal Psychology. Her work transformed my life and molded many of my ideas about transpersonal psychology. I had the opportunity to create, develop, and work with Barbara, her staff, and thousands of students over the years. My training at the school was extensive and fostered my leadership skills. From 1994 to 2000, I served as the Department Head of Healing Science and from 2000 to 2005 as the Dean of Year Four Studies. In addition, I created the Brennan Integration Program that trained graduates and teachers to supervise healers around the world. If I was ever given a spiritual mentor in this lifetime, I would consider Barbara this person. I spent eighteen years under her guidance and mentoring before retiring from the school to write and be with my family. I feel blessed and restored through the work I did with her and for the school.

Coming Full Circle: Another Turn on the Path

In the last five years of my teaching for the Brennan School, I often heard a voice that would ask me to read Mark 2 or Isaiah 12:2. I thought, "What in the world is happening to me? I am not a fundamentalist Christian. We are not teaching the Bible here. What do you want from me?" I argued with God: "Don't you have someone better, someone who is more knowledgeable about the Bible—a theologian perhaps, a rabbi, or a nun? For heaven's sake, I am at the top of my game here." Yet the more I struggled, the more I was guided and told to read the Bible. On several occasions, I noticed biblical principles being taught alongside what I was teaching. I was asked several times to read certain passages in the Bible. These passages directly related to healing.

I continued arguing with God until one night I heard a voice say, "Donna, you have read so many books, but you have never read the Bible. I want you to read it with new eyes. Read it from the perspective of the spiritual journey of the family and God Realization."

Of course I resisted and argued, saying "I just want to tell you I am not a fundamentalist Christian. I found my own path studying and teaching healing science. I don't even believe parts of the creation story." But soon I came to realize that *resistance was futile. I would be assimilated into the written word of Scripture—whether I liked it or not.*

This book is a culmination of that journey. It unravels the mystery within our Family Tree of Knowledge and restores hope for those who feel lost on their path. And it will rejuvenate those who want to embody Scripture in a new way.

Part 1:

Chapter 1: Realizing God within the Family

In the first chapter, I set the groundwork for the God Realization Process and your journey through reading this book. You will understand how your Family Tree of Knowledge affects your life today. We will explore how current brain research is instrumental in supporting our healing process. Understanding how our brain operates and stores information is important if we are to transform our generational negative love bonds into positive ones. I believe our brains are naturally wired for God's immanent love and grace. When we are not mirrored in our true essence, our brains can and often do program the experience as a negative love bond.

Our love actually bonds with either positive or negative experiences that set the stage for all of our relationships. In these pages, you'll learn that the Ten Spiritual Keys (Commandments) are the covenant with God that secures our healthy physical, psychological, interpersonal, and spiritual development. Without this knowledge, we can adapt to any unhealthy situation and, on an unconscious level, mistakenly believe this negative situation is love. People are meant to bond together out of unity and oneness, but when this capacity is suppressed, our potential to express our true nature is suppressed. We'll discuss the four basic principles for health and well-being, which involve putting God first, our partner and family second, our work and creative process third, and our community fourth. When we are out of balance with this wisdom, our life can become chaotic and lose its sense of true meaning.

Chapter 2: Faith Required

In Chapter Two, we explore how faith is a universal quality that guides us toward the greater mystery of who we are and the meaning of our lives. Our faith drives us forward to overcome obstacles and to find true peace and happiness. In this chapter, we look at the meaning of faith and how it affects your life. You were guided by faith to pick up this book and continue reading, in hopes of finding another clue or answer to your path toward wholeness and unity. Our faith is important in building healthy relationships with our partner, our children, and our community. Faith is what guides us into deeper, eternal levels of intimacy and trust.

Chapter 3: The God-Realization Genogram

In Chapter Three, you'll learn how to create your own God-Realization Genogram using your Family Tree of Knowledge and the Ten Spiritual Keys. You'll use a traditional genogram symbol chart to identify both positive and negative love bonds in your family and explore how your negative love bonds correspond to transgressions in one or more of the Keys.

Chapter 4: The Ten Spiritual Keys

In Chapter Four, we will look at the Ten Spiritual Keys (Commandments) and discuss why God instructs us to write them on our hearts, souls, eyes, and hands, as noted by the points of light in the accompanying illustration. We'll explore the importance of teaching the Keys to our children and writing them on the doorposts of our homes. The Keys were meant to purify our hearts, our souls, our eyes, and our hands, to help us master our impulses or the unbridled energy within us (some call this energy *the serpent*). We learn how to use the Keys to open our relationship with God within us before bringing this experience into our human relationships. Moreover, we consider why Christ reduced these Keys to two: to simplify the process and welcome everyone into the Kingdom of God.

Part 2: The Ten Spiritual Keys

In Chapters 5 to 14, you can explore each of the Ten Commandments as Ten Spiritual Keys to healing your life and family today. You'll awaken the God-Realization Process and heal the generational negative love bonds that hold you hostage to the past. You'll discover that each Key represents a doorway into your personal relationship with God and then builds the bridge for your relationships with your partner, your family, and your community.

The Keys relate to the Ten Commandments as follows:

The Ten Keys Are...	The Ten Commandments Are...
The Key to Wholeness	You shall have no other gods before me.
The Key to Fulfillment	You shall not make any graven images.
The Key to Meaning	You shall not misuse the name of the Lord your God.
The Key to Peace	You shall make the Sabbath holy.
The Key to Belonging	You shall honor your mother and father.
The Key to Respecting Life	You shall not kill.
The Key to Unity	You shall not commit adultery.
The Key to Potential	You shall not steal.
The Key to Ourselves	You shall not bear false witness.
The Key to Manifestation	You shall not covet.

You will learn how to work with each Key by placing it on your heart, soul, eyes, and hands, and why it is important to teach them to your children. We will explore these Sacred Keys and why this information is important to healing your family today. You will unlock the greatest mystery, open yourself to blessings from a thousand generations, and release the generational negative love bonds that hold you hostage to the past.

Part 3: Next Steps

Chapter 15: Restoring Your Divine Qualities

In this final section, you'll learn about the seven main Divine qualities that reside in each of us. You will learn how to restore each of the Divine qualities that may have been suppressed in you. The

Spiritual Keys and the Divine qualities work together to help you heal your negative love bonds and express your Divine potential. I will also introduce the *I AM* Meditation as a way to release your negative love bonds and restore each quality. This process is an integration of Biblical principles, psychology, and Brennan Healing Science methodology.

The Divine Qualities are:

Divine Trust
Divine Self-Love and Self-Acceptance
Divine Respect
Divine Interpersonal Love
Divine Communication
Divine Vision
Divine Wisdom

Each quality opens you to reach your Divine potential in any given moment. The corresponding *I AM* mantras help you to release your negative beliefs and the emotions that hold you hostage to the past. Your cone of perception widens as you restore each quality. When you use the *I AM* Meditation, the mantras help you challenge your faulty belief systems and reprogram your brain and deep limbic system toward the Divine within you. You'll see in the accompanying illustration how each mantra connects with a point of light within you, beginning at the lowest point of the belly and working its way up the core of your being.

The I AM mantras are:

I Know Divine Wisdom from the *I AM that I AM*
I See Divine Truth from the *I AM that I AM*
I Communicate Truth from the *I AM that I AM*
I Relate to Others from the *I AM that I AM*
I Respect the *I AM that I AM*
I Love and Accept the *I AM that I AM*
I Trust in the *I AM that I AM*

Working with each mantra will ultimately lead you to trust in your Divine potential from the I AM that I AM. You can close each meditation with the mantra, "I trust in my Divine potential from the I AM that I AM." After reading this section, you can learn more about the *I AM* Meditation in my book, *Restoring Our Divine Nature: The* I *AM Meditation Workbook,* or visit my website (www. livingfromgrace.com).

After exploring my own family heritage and finding out the truth about my maternal and paternal ancestors, I feel enlivened by the experience. I have learned that regardless of our situation, God seeks us and wants us to know Him. I can now put the branches back on my family tree and feel rooted in the *Garden of oneness* with our Creator. I found that my tree has a rich heritage with branches reaching into Christianity and Judaism. In 1864, one of my grandfathers, Edward Lyon Clark, was the warden of the Christ Church in Philadelphia. Other branches of the tree have a long history of names such as Paul I, II, and III, Peter, and James. It is exciting to reclaim my ancestral heritage while healing the generational negative love bonds within the family tree. You too will find the beauty within your Family Tree of Knowledge. I promise the exploration will be worth it!

PART 1

OUR FAMILY TREE OF KNOWLEDGE

Chapter 1

Realizing God Within the Family

Embracing and healing our Family Tree of Knowledge is our journey home into oneness with God.

The sacredness of the family spiritual journey begins, and rightfully so, with the oldest story told in the Bible. We learn from this story that in the beginning, Adam and Eve stood naked before God without fear or shame (Genesis 2:25), as pure as the luminosity of God's unified love, seeing only God's blessings and grace. But when they listened to the serpent's words over the words of God, their relationship with God and the unified field of God's love was changed. By forsaking God's only Commandment, they betrayed God—and their deepest selves. They suddenly felt the need to lie, blame, and deny responsibility, and they began to uncover the mystery of the knowledge of good and evil. They would move from the spiritual world into the physical world.

With veils of separation now covering their eyes, Adam and Eve recognized their differences and wanted to hide themselves from each other and from God. They found fig leaves to cover their nakedness, which was a symbol of their individuality and descent into the physical world. They could now learn to discern the difference between good and evil, blessings and calamity. They were now responsible for their choices and the outcomes. As they tried to hide and then talked to God, Adam and Eve's behavior revealed their veils of illusion. Instead of seeing only unity, they now experienced separation, differences, and divisiveness: Adam blamed Eve, and Eve blamed the serpent. It was no longer possible to stay in the Garden of oneness with God. By turning away from God to follow their own desires, Adam and Eve had fallen from immortality and unified love into duality and illusion. God clothed them in skin and they became earthbound. They were sent out of the Garden of Eden to create their own family. Eve would now bear children while Adam would work the land. Their Family Tree of Knowledge would become our journey home to oneness with God.

In the fractured family relationships of today, you might see yourself or your family members suffering these same symptoms of disconnect that Adam and Eve felt. The experience of being banished from the garden mirrors the same journey and pain that is experienced when a family member becomes an outcast or a scapegoat. On your own journey, personality and character flaws (such as blaming others for your shortcomings) can be unconscious ways to cover internal and external feelings of separation from God. To heal these fractures and the separation, it makes sense that our first steps must be toward God. The journey home will be one of listening, prayer, and forgiveness, and it will provide us with hope, direction, and enlightenment toward communion with God. That unity is what I call *God-Realization*. Attaining God-Realization is the foundation for healing a family—and it is our goal in this book.

The God-Realization Process

Our search for truth, a deeper knowing of God, and the answer to the age-old question, "Who am I ?" will require us to again become naked, uncovered, and undefended before God's omnipotent grace, love, and luminosity. Surrendering our separation, blaming, vanity, arrogance, defenses, and sinful nature, as well as taking responsibility for our actions, words, and deeds are key requirements to finding God's grace and compassion and releasing the blessings from a thousand generations.

On our journey toward God-Realization, we are meant to walk a certain path in the world, but each personal journey is unique. You are the only one who can dissolve the illusions that separate you from God. Spiritual leaders, teachers, psychotherapists, energy healing practitioners, or complete strangers may guide you toward the mystery behind the journey, but it is you who must make the ultimate choice to integrate your negative splits and embrace spiritual wholeness. Hidden beneath the veils of your perceptions, the immanent light calls you home. Your sweet surrender to the journey—embracing with love all that emerges, both positive and negative, and listening to the still, small voice that guides you—will lead you to knowing the greater mystery. This journey will help you to unravel the mysteries of your family and ultimately to find your spiritual destiny.

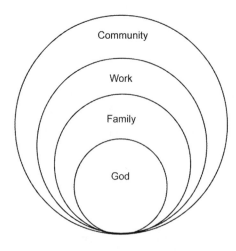

The image above illustrates the path in its simplest form. First, you must focus on your core, where you must connect with and claim your Divine heritage within. You are the light, and knowing this will support your very being. Second, you will bring that light into relationship with your partner and cultivate a Divine oneness that will include your children and then the rest of your family. Third, you will foster and bring your light and wisdom to your career choice and passion. And finally, you will serve your community from a place of balance and Divine service. You'll soon discover that when you are fully grounded and your life is balanced, the power of living in right order moves from your core Divinity outwards. However, when these four pieces are out of order, your life can become chaotic, leaving you, your family, your work, and your life imbalanced. For example, if you spend more time at work than with your family, your family life will suffer from the loss of your presence and guidance.

The key to maintaining the balance lies in our core—with maintaining our connection to Divinity. When issues turn up, this is most likely because a separation happened there first. It was the same with Adam and Eve. As they fell from immortality and omnipotent oneness, they forgot their deep connection with their Maker. Now the process of remembering our Divine roots and our true immortality will come from learning once again how to listen to and follow God's voice. At the same time, we must also master our own self-doubt and negative thoughts and feelings.

To accomplish this, we will use the God-Realization Process. You may consider this process a map for your spiritual journey. It involves four necessary requirements:

An understanding of positive and negative love bonds

An understanding of the Ten Spiritual Keys (Commandments)

A willingness to delve into your family history, with the above in mind

An understanding of the seven Divine qualities

Positive and Negative Love Bonds

To begin the God-Realization Process, we must first have an understanding of *positive love bonds* and *negative love bonds* and how they manifest in our lives. Negative love bonds form when reenactments, both conscious and unconscious, of negative family and ancestral patterns—such as addictions, infidelity, or chronic anxiety—disconnect us from one or more of God's Commandments. From a spiritual and psychological perspective, a positive love bond forms when a mother and father both infuse their child's consciousness with grace and love. They provide the security, love and respect that lays the foundation for the child's physiological, psychological, and spiritual health and well-being.

The center (or ground) of the child's consciousness—self-realization and God-realization—can be anchored in the luminosity of God's grace and love as a positive love bond. Or it can be anchored in neglect, abuse, anxiety, and depression as a negative love bond. Directly imprinted into the consciousness of our cellular membrane, positive and negative love bonds are transmitted from and can be traced back through our families, often for generations. Our biblical ancestors provided us with Spiritual Keys that enable us to embrace our positive love bonds, heal our negative love bonds, and live healthy and fruitful lives connected to the grace of God. The Ten Commandments given to Moses at Mount Sinai were meant to be inscribed into the very fabric of our consciousness to ensure our personal relationship with God.

There is a scientific aspect to this as well. Modern research shows concrete links between our ancestors, our emotions, and our very being. In fact, Dr. Daniel G. Amen MD, a clinical neuroscientist and psychiatrist, invites us to consider that our brain is actually "the hardware to our soul." All of our knowledge and the wisdom of our Divine potential is processed within our brains and transmitted to all of our other senses and body systems. Dr. Amen notes that if the brain doesn't work well because it is plagued with automatic negative thoughts (ANTS), the soul cannot truly be expressed. In one of Amen's lectures, he says (and I paraphrase his words): *It is not that the person's soul doesn't want to express its Divine beauty; it is that the malfunctions in the brain don't allow it.* He suggests several types of treatment for changing negative brain patterns, from medication to meditation and prayer.

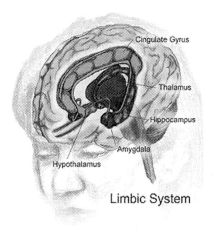

Limbic System

Let's go a little further down this scientific path. Most of us know that our genetic code (DNA) is passed down to us from our maternal and paternal families. Bruce H. Lipton PhD, a former medical professor, research scientist, and cell biologist, has discovered that DNA is actually influenced by the membrane or tissue that surrounds it and can also be affected by positive and negative thoughts. In his book, *The Biology of Belief: Unleashing the Power of Consciousness, Matter, and Miracles*, Lipton suggests that our cells carry other awareness beyond the genetic code, and the state of our consciousness affects our cells' health. Investigating our familial story becomes even more important when we think about the direct impact our ancestors have upon our cells.

Our most basic emotions, memories, and instincts develop within the brain in what is called the *limbic system*. This tiny part of the brain developed to accommodate bonding, feeding, and reproductive fight-or-flight responses. The limbic system coordinates the behavioral, autonomic (involuntary), and hormonal adjustments required to maintain homeostasis or normal operation. When humans experience the basic emotions of love, pleasure, hunger, or fear, the limbic system releases neurohormones throughout the body, and changes occur in the heart and immune system. For example, when a child smells her mother (through the olfactory nerve and the limbic system), the child responds with both cardio-respiratory and GI-related activity. In other words, her emotional and visceral nervous systems are directly affected by any interaction with her parents (Ruggiero, David PhD). Simply put, the brain's connection to basic emotions influences each cell through hormonal or chemical reactions.

Here's another example: An infant is bumped and cries, feeling pain. If the mother instantly picks him up and soothes him by rocking him closely, the baby associates soft touch, words, and love with less pain. But if the mother soothes the baby by feeding him even though he's not hungry, the baby associates food with less pain, which sets up a negative bond—needing food to reduce pain—for the future. Repetitions of these need–response interactions become literally imbedded, or wired, within our cellular memory.

Research by philosopher Eva Jablonka and biologist Marion Lamb, as presented in their 1995 book, *Epigenetic Inheritance and Evolution: The Lamarckian Dimension*, suggests that genes are far more fluid and responsive to the environment than we have realized. Information can be transmitted to *descendants* in other ways than the base sequence of DNA. Interactions are stored in the cellular membrane of a newborn baby.

Our brains record this bonding in the deep limbic system. Using the chemicals of love and bonding for survival, a recycled negative event is recorded in the brain as love based on fear, replacing a more positive bond of love based on nurturance, security, and trust. Unraveling the mystery of our familial and ancestral heritage allows us to recover our spiritual heritage and frees us from bondage to the negative patterns passed down generationally.

We also increase our well-being as we reconnect with our Divinity. As Andrew Newberg MD and Mark Robert Waldman write in their book, *How God Changes Your Brain: Breakthrough Findings from a Leading Neuroscientist,* the brain responds positively to spiritual influences. They researched six different structures of the brain to understand how God and spirituality affects the brain. Their groundbreaking research identifies how our concept of God affects our frontal lobe, limbic system, anterior cingulate gyrus, amygdale, thalamus, and parietal lobe. They suggest that *the more we meditate and pray, the more likely we are to experience a mystical or transcendental state,* and that these states can be measured by taking SPECT brain scans during these peak experiences. Our belief in God, as well as our images, prayers, and meditation practices, activate different areas of our brains and cause different mystical experiences.

I believe the brain responds because we are unlocking a certain part of ourselves. When we do so, we release our negative thoughts, feelings, and behaviors as well as the crooked paths from generational negative love bonds. This process frees us to receive the blessings of a thousand generations and to offer these blessings to our children and the world.

Unraveling this greater mystery is our true birthright. Our brain is actually wired for God or what we call spiritual experiences. By suppressing this vital information, we miss an essential key to spiritual enlightenment. When Moses freed his people from bondage, their journey involved more than personal freedom. They also needed to free their minds from Egyptian ways and thoughts to restore their relationship with God and find their spiritual roots.

Moses' quest to restore his people led him to the top of Mount Sinai where he had a direct experience of God-Realization and received the Ten Spiritual Keys to restore the health and spiritual well-being of his people. Even today, these keys are necessary to restore our Divine nature and secure our communion with God.

The Ten Spiritual Keys

Certainly, you are already familiar with the *Ten Spiritual Keys*; you just know them by another name: the Ten Commandments. I prefer to think of the Commandments as Spiritual Keys because in my teaching I've found a lot of resistance to the Commandments. People tend to see them as a set of restrictive, outdated rules, and sadly, that's the way they've often been presented to us. Cross-culturally, these Commandments, universal truths, values, or codes of ethics are the foundation and tenets of all the major religions. They are universally accepted because, when followed, they bring peace and harmony to the individual and to the societies in which we live. Though they may be presented very differently, all spiritual traditions dovetail with these accepted ideas. But the primary reason for the Commandments—communication with God—is overlooked while focusing on the "moral society" aspect instead. Therefore, these rules or moral codes become a punishment, something to push up against rather than a way to walk with and listen to God from within.

Clearing our inner relationship with God will always lead us into peace and harmony with our family and society. In this book, we will review the Ten Commandments or Spiritual Keys as a way to open the door to communication with God within you. As we do this, we begin to understand how we have mapped both positive and negative love bonds into our very wiring, perceptions, and life experiences. I invite you to turn your thoughts away from a set of rules that control society to a set of Keys that exist to unlock or awaken the Divine within you and to increase your communication with God. If these words do not resonate with you or your religious or cultural tradition, please find ones that work for you and practice with your own words and universal truths.

We will give each key its own chapter in this book. You'll be able to explore it from a modern viewpoint and understand its relevance in your life today. Remember, the Keys are to open you to the light within, to sustain your direct communication with God, and to tame the unbridled life force, the serpent or Id, that rests at the base of your spine.

The Secrets of Our Ancestors

Historically, the nuclear family system—the primary family relationship—defines the self and our relationship to our Divine (God-centered) heritage. Each of us has a history of familial, ancestral, and cultural wounds that have led us to the path of self-understanding and enlightenment. You may have felt suppressed by parts of your family heritage and labeled the pattern *dysfunctional*. Without understanding how to free yourself, you may have tried hard not to repeat the unwanted behavior or concluded that you were doomed to repeat the same patterns.

But the good news is, we can trace our spiritual heritage and unravel the mystery of who we are as evolving spiritual beings by embracing the path of our parents and ancestors. If we learn how to recognize and embrace both our positive and negative experiences with insight, love and acceptance, forgiveness and compassion, we can find the path that will lead us toward true peace and satisfaction.

Uncovering and healing the crooked paths of our families is part of our spiritual journey and our return to the Divine within. Letting go of our previous woundedness, which inhibits reunion and communion with God, restores our ability to accept and forgive the faults of others and to reclaim our spiritual heritage. By taking this spiritual journey of finding and healing the negative love bonds and their consequences in our lives and our families, we become not only self-realized, but God-realized.

When Adam and Eve left the Garden of Eden, they embarked on creating their own family. Their family tree would encompass all of Adam's and Eve's choices, as well as their original connection to the Source. Understanding the importance of the family tree can unlock its great wisdom and knowledge from within and connect us to our spiritual heritage. In this process, our family tree is our own Tree of the Knowledge of Good and Evil.

The Family Tree of Knowledge

The *Family Tree of Knowledge* represents the forces of consciousness held deep within our nervous system, an intricate web of communication between all systems of the body and brain. As I discussed earlier, this nervous system holds all the wisdom and knowledge passed down through the generations, mapped into our genes and consciousness from both of our biological parents and passed on as transmissions of consciousnesses from other parental sources, such as adoptive parents. The transmission of consciousness from an adoptive parent or caregiver onto the membrane surrounding the DNA is as effective as the contributing consciousness passed on genetically. However, we know very little about what has been imprinted into our genes and consciousness. We tend to focus more on health issues and what physical illnesses or conditions may have been passed down in the family, but spiritual breaches can have just as many—or more—negative effects than an illness or health defect. We also talk about these spiritual imprints less, leaving them to fall into the shadows of the past as family secrets.

Mastering the knowledge and secrets held within our Family Tree of Knowledge becomes our spiritual journey here on Earth. To help us with this endeavor, we will use a tool called the *God-Realization Genogram*. This genogram (which I'll describe in detail in Chapter 3) is an easy way for you to explore your family experiences and see where you must focus your spiritual energy for healing and understanding. You will use prayer and meditation as your tools. Your goal will be to restore the *seven Divine qualities*, one or more of which may be covered or suppressed within you because of the secrets or breaches. You'll learn more about these qualities later, but for now, just know they are essential aspects to your very being; your Divine qualities make you what you are.

As you'll see in the pages of this book, each family story gives us insight into the fabric of human nature and the struggle with these concepts. The keys to mastering the knowledge within our family heritage—both good and evil—are laid out within the stories of our ancestors' journey. Mastering your family heritage and your family issues opens you up to the blessings of a thousand generations.

Chapter 2

Faith Required

Build your life on faith, not fear. ~Dr. Michael Beckwith

Any spiritual process or journey must begin with faith. The Bible tells us many times how important faith is, even if it is *"as small as a mustard seed."* Hebrews 11:1 says, *"Now faith is being sure of what we hope for and certain of what we do not see."* On one level, faith can be as simple as sheer, unadulterated belief—the unending certitude that God's immanent grace, light, and love is the foundation of your being. But on another level, we make faith much more complicated by confusing it with ego and the things that ego wants to hold onto. Our faith can be skewed when our underlying motives are based in fear. Sometimes our faith is steadfast and other times it's embroiled with our own images, defenses, and fears.

However, the clearer we are about faith, the easier it will be for us to connect with the seven Divine qualities and restore them in our lives. As with the Divine qualities, faith is innate in every person. It is the basis for every emotion we feel and every action we take. You have to have faith in order to trust the people in your relationships. You have to have faith to drive down the street, believing everyone else will obey the traffic rules. You have to have faith in order to try what I'm putting forth in this book. When you picked up this book, you must have had some kind of faith that it would open your awareness to something, even if you weren't sure what that something was.

Because we're acting on faith in one way or another, faith—still a complicated concept—is more accessible to us every single day. Inside each of us is the Divine kernel of faith. Our Divine nature actually provides us with an innate sense of faith, of knowing or believing in something larger than ourselves that is responsible for the world around us and the universe we live in. Faith arises from deep within and gives us hope in the midst of crisis. It leads us onto a spiritual path of seeking to answer the age-old question, "Who am I?"

Faith is also a powerful mode of connection, acting as a type of healing for those who have lost their way or are in despair. This is why we'll often describe a person in difficulty as having lost their faith. Faith can be hidden beneath a myriad of pain and sorrow. In these cases, another's faith is needed to help restore that of the person in pain and bring about hope. How many times, either in real life or in a movie, have you heard a friend or family member tell a person in crisis, "I believe in you" or "I have faith in you"? Their faith serves as a foundation on which the person in crisis can connect and begin to rebuild their own—and heal as a result.

Faith and the God-Realization Process

Christ's message does the same thing for us. His message was one of faith, and it leads us to reach out and help those in need because, through those actions, we connect others to faith as well. We are faith builders in the world, and the message is clear: to "love one another as you love yourself." Loving ourselves can only mature when we are directly in tune with the God within us.

Our ability to access faith and communicate with the Divine within us is our gift to our life companion and family members. Our faith provides the foundation for bringing the Holy Spirit into all of our relationships. The healing we hope to bring to our families through this process is grounded in our ability to demonstrate our faith. When we step out to explore the positive and negative love bonds of our family ancestry, we give weight and leadership by showing our belief that the family stands for something more than just a random collection of people thrown together by DNA. In seeking to reconnect with God, we hope to connect with that "something more" and fully express the positive aspects of everything the family can be, leaving behind the negative ones that have only held it back.

I should note here that the way you show faith to your family will not always be "religious." Many relationships today are a blend of different cultural backgrounds, religious beliefs, and family traditions. These differences offer us the opportunity to grow and expand the way we see the world to include another's life experiences. Sharing the richness of our varying cultural, religious, and familial backgrounds can enhance our relationships or complicate them. For some families, it is easy to include these differences and adapt; in others, rigid rules can limit the ability to embrace another's experience and beliefs in life. Nevertheless, we need to show how faith goes beyond culture, religion, and family traditions. We have an innate knowledge that we are connected to something larger than us.

Paul's letter to the Galatians focused on faith as the gift from Christ. Faith releases us from bondage to Jewish law, rules, and regulations. Paul preached that our faith in Christ dissolved the barriers of separation and unified communities to receive the Holy Spirit and become one with God. Faith restored hope for the Gentiles and brought peace to unsettling times. It was by faith that the Gentiles were guided to enter the Kingdom of Heaven and receive the teaching of Jesus Christ—not by adhering to Jewish law.

Clearly, no one is justified before God by the law, because, "The righteous will live by faith." The law is not based on faith; on the contrary, "The man who does these things will live by them." ~Galatians 3:11-12

Therefore, we must not confuse faith with religion or laws. Religion is a way in which someone can explore their faith, but faith goes beyond religious laws. It is innate in every person regardless of religion, culture, or tradition. Paul's message invites us to look at how holding onto rigid rules and laws could limit our connection with the Holy Spirit. Although the laws were important, they were merely guideposts toward finding God. Faith in God or Christ is the universal connection for all people. You can go to any place on any continent and find faith and hope in people. People express that faith every day. It may be as simple as faith in a better day tomorrow.

When we help others who are in need, we're helping them with their faith. Some may say, "It's my religion," because Christ said to help others, but look at what happens during catastrophes like those in Haiti or New Orleans. Strangers from all walks of life become very connected to one another and have faith that they can rebuild their cities and their families. When these disasters happen, people, religious or not, come out to help each other.

Sharing Faith with Our Life Companion

Finding faith within and sharing it with our partner builds a strong spiritual field and base for our family. When two people share from the Divine within them, the greater mystery of their relationship is revealed. The light within each is recognized and respected. We are able to provide comfort and understanding in times of pain and sorrow. We rely on Divine wisdom in the times of forgiveness and help each other to grow and heal. We are committed to work with each other on our weaknesses, shortcomings, and failures. We find truth and healing from within. We explore our different family heritages together and find the faith that we can unravel the greater mystery for the healing of our family.

Faith can lead us in new directions and provide us with hope when, as a couple, we are faced with the inevitable challenges of life. Its guiding light leads us through the dark times and illumines us in the good times. When we have strong faith in God, our faith in each other can grow stronger. And it provides the foundation for our children to learn about the Divine within them.

We had a particularly trying time in my family when my husband was going through hardship with his family's business. He had been in the business for thirty-five years, but when his uncle died and his father retired, everything fell apart and Jeff's relatives pulled it out from under him. This was his life's work. He fell from grace and into dark places he didn't speak to me about. When he lost his faith, he relied on his ego. He began trying to fix things on his own, trying to hide things and refusing to talk about them. When things broke open about what he was actually doing, he had lost thirty pounds and made himself sick. He was not relying on God and our relationship; instead, he was relying on his fear and his doubt.

At that point, Jeff was sure I was going to leave him. I told him clearly this was not going to destroy us, and it was my faith in him that brought him back to find himself in the way he was before his fall from grace. He had convinced himself I would leave him and created this big mess in his mind and in our finances. Most people would be filing for divorce under such circumstances, but I said, "Whatever this is, it isn't you, and I won't let it destroy us." It was my faith in him and the Divine within him that helped him let go of what he was doing and come into honesty with himself and his fears. Before that, he was acting out of character and had lost connection to his integrity, but all the while I was telling him, "I believe in something bigger than what you are connected to right now."

Note that what I am saying here isn't about putting your religion on someone. This is about faith in what is within us. That's one big reason why I think there are so many divorces. When our partners fall from grace—maybe lose their sense of self or break one of the Spiritual Keys—a lot of shame comes up. When you're rooted in the other person instead of the Divine, you react to your world being destroyed. You feel betrayed and your trust is broken. Your world, beliefs, and images about your life and the other person come crashing down around you. The ego gets involved, and your faith is more embroiled with focusing on your security, your identity, and your standing in the world. You're not connected to the "something more" that your relationship could be grounded in. But when you are rooted in God first, you believe in the Divine and your relationship is grounded in that, not in your partner's fall from grace. This is where I believe our partnerships lack understanding and guidance from the beginning. We need to build our relationship on the rock of God first. In this way, we honor our relationship by maintaining integrity. We can never truly be destroyed by our partner's fall from grace. They may have lost our trust and respect, yet we are grounded in our faith. One way to show faith is to believe in our partner beyond their faults. If *both people* in a relationship attempted to do this, the divorce rate would likely go down.

Another opportunity comes up if your partner is getting ready to go out for a job interview. Perhaps they have doubts and are thinking or saying, "Why would they hire me? I'm not worthy. I've lost my edge." When you talk to your partner, remind them of their gifts and talents that might help them land the job. A partner who has faith will go beyond negative self-talk and remind you of the part of you that wants to be lived rather than the negative that's trying to sabotage your life.

Your faith also gets expressed when you join together with your partner about certain ideas, thoughts, and beliefs as a foundation for your home. You join your light together to build the energy and consciousness for your family *mind field*, the field of energy between you and your family members. You are saying that your home is filled with unconditional love and that everyone will be respected and forgiven for their shortcomings. Your faith in the Divine within each person is stronger that any shortcomings or failures that anyone might experience. It's similar to having communion, but in this instance, it is a communion of two people coming together and expanding the light within your relationship. You and your partner become one without shame.

You and your partner become one and united from the Divine within. Both of you have made choices to build your home on the "Rock of God" with the foundation made from trust in the God within each other, humble love and acceptance of each other's gifts as well as shortcomings, and respect for the Divine in all sentient life. These very basic qualities provide the foundation for your children to lead healthy, happy, productive lives. They also open the doorway of your hearts for other relationships, because people who come into your grace- and love-filled home will feel safe and respected. That shows your faith in something higher than each of you, as well as faith in your relationship.

Sharing Faith with Our Children

Likewise, the faith in your relationship is passed on and shared with your children. Faith is fundamental to our children's physical, emotional, intellectual, interpersonal, and spiritual well-being. Your faith reflects your child's Divine nature—you're reflecting and teaching that God lives within them, and this gives children the opportunity to live from their innate nature. It reflects the truth of who they are and offers them the hope and opportunity to have a God-realized sense of identity. Children are naturally undefended and emanate God's grace and love. They are innocent and full of light, not too far from their unique Divine nature. Their innocence and honesty flows most naturally from them. The more we learn to mirror their Divine nature, the less this knowledge falls from their awareness. Our respect for the Divine within them helps to build their deep sense of knowing God within and ignites their faith.

When we mirror trust in God to our children, essentially showing them the example of our faith, their self-love and respect in their own faith can grow. They have the inner strength and power to stand strong in their times of adversity. The Divine qualities preserve our children's faith, whereas mistrust, self-judgments, and a lack of self-respect can diminish it. For example, children who are abused are often overwhelmed with feelings of despair and a deep sense of loneliness. Their unique sense of self is buried beneath years of negative experiences. Moreover, they can lose faith in a whirlpool of unsettling feelings and images. They adapt and bond with the negativity around them in order to survive. Their faith bonds with the hope that life can be different and they can ultimately be loved. Their faith becomes bonded with an idealized image of what perfect love would feel like. This misconception can lead them to seek perfect love and be devastated when it doesn't occur. Their faith becomes attached to another rather than God within. The child or adult learns to look outside of themselves. When this happens, trust bonds to the "other" first, instead of to the God within.

Understand that building faith within our family arises from creating positive love bonds with our children, so they feel secure and heard. This is not an easy task these days when families rarely have time to get together, even around the dinner table. Most families are on the go, eating fast food out, often apart and at different times, rushing from one meeting or practice or activity to another. There's a belief that success is bonding: The more I do for you, the more material things I give you, and the more opportunities I give you, the better chance you have to be a whole, well-rounded person. Yet we're finding out that this is a false assumption. At one of my conferences, with 700 healers in the room, I asked, "How many of you eat at home five times a week?" No one raised a hand. "Three times a week?" No one. "How many of you ever eat at home with your families?" Only two or three of 700 healers raised their hands.

When you don't share meals with your family, you're missing the opportunity to communicate to your children that "this family is important, and you are an important part of the whole. I want to hear about your day and respect what you have to say." It's all about building faith, self-esteem, and respect. Creating a family dinner ritual provides a healthy foundation for you and your children to communicate. Over the years, as your children become young adults, they will always feel comfortable to talk and share with you. The positive love bonds of trust, love and acceptance, and respect become the family mind field, where your children can always relax and feel safe enough to share their deepest thoughts and emotions.

When we learn to listen to God within, we can learn to listen to the God within our children. Sometimes we listen from our own cone of perception, our own limited viewpoint. We hear what we want to hear rather than what they're saying or the broader perception of what's happening in their lives. When children experience a difficult day, they need to share it in a safe, trusted environment where their voice will be heard and accepted. You may not have thought of it this way, yet listening well is an essential component that supports our children's ability to have faith.

Faith and Healing

In the Bible, Christ often speaks of faith and healing. In the story of the woman who touched His robes and was healed, Christ stopped to ask, "Who touched me?" He could feel the person's faith pulling on his energy. He could feel his consciousness for healing going out of Him. He told the woman, "It's your faith that has made you whole." In all healing, it is our faith that brings wholeness. Whether it's faith in our therapist, faith in a spouse, or faith in a healer, if we don't have faith that the healing will work, most of the time it won't. It's not that the healer is not doing great work; it's that the doubting consciousness of the person is blocking their own healing; they lack the faith in the healer or themselves or in God.

You'll find that doing this process of moving toward God-Realization is the same as with any other healing process. It's our faith in the God-Realization Process that will bring us back to healing with God and bring healing into our families. You can't do much without it. Often, the lack of faith in your own healing process can create a barrier of resistance that blocks the light within you from shining forth. For example, in my private practice some clients come for healing only to appease a friend or family member, yet don't believe they have the power to heal, so the session can fall flat. In these situations, the person usually has a negative love bond, a belief that sets up a barrier of resistance to taking in the love and healing work.

Do you have such a barrier? Think of it this way: When someone says a loving compliment to you, how do you receive it? Many will reject it and not take it inside. You might push it out and simply say it's untrue, or maybe you laugh it off. You may not allow yourself to take it into your heart and body and to be nourished by positive compliments. Believe it or not, some of us are wired to take in negative insults and criticisms more than positive compliments. It's the same thing when someone is sending healing work or prayer. If you won't take it in, you can't benefit from it. But when our faith makes us whole, it opens a doorway for that consciousness and energy to permeate the barriers and to go beyond our limited sense of self. Rather than rejecting it because we feel we don't deserve to be forgiven or don't believe we can be healed, in faith we feel we do deserve it and can allow the energy to come inside.

To begin exploring the status and strength of your faith, ask yourself these questions:

Am I open and able to receive love and healing?

Where in my life have I been connected to my faith? Did it bring me wholeness or bring me through a crisis?

What is my faith in my partner like, and did it ever bring me or my partner through a crisis?

Have I ever had faith in my child(ren) at a time when he/she/they were struggling with something? How did my faith help them through?

Think of the times when goodness or healing has been offered to you. Did you push it away or take it into your heart naturally and genuinely?

Maybe you don't have examples of faith in your life, or maybe you had faith and your family fell apart anyway. That's okay! You can still have the Spirit working in your life. Please do not feel yourself in judgment here. Things often don't work out despite our best intentions because conditions are not always optimal. Our lives are not always in ideal places. Often, what we want for ourselves and our families will fall short. The question is: How will we allow the Divine to work through us when we must get through it? How do we bring the light within us to our children when our lives are falling apart? You might feel hopelessness, but, as Dante says, *"When you walk through the door of hopelessness, you find hope at the other end."* You have to walk through the hopelessness to rejuvenate your hope or your faith. Sometimes you have to look at all these different parts of yourself to find your faith again.

The best place to start is by exploring yourself. Get curious about the here and now. Something brought you to this book. Whether you call it faith or not, something drew you to explore yourself. Follow that inclination, even if it's just a small one. There is something driving you here, wanting you to discover new territory in yourself. Call it curiosity if you must give it a name. Start there. Eventually, you'll be able to map out your own way back to faith.

Chapter 3

The God-Realization Genogram

If you look deeply into the palm of your hand, you will see your parents and all generations of your ancestors. All of them are alive in this moment. Each is present in your body. You are the continuation of each of these people. ~Thich Nhat Hanh

Each of you are now invited to unravel the mystery of your heritage by learning how to trace the positive and negative love bonds in your family and to pray and listen to God. You'll do this with an important tool that we've already mentioned: the God-Realization Genogram. If you've never heard of a genogram before, it might help you to think first of a family tree, an image most people are familiar with.

The family tree is a diagram that outlines our ancestral heritage. In a systems approach to family therapy, we use a version of a family tree called a Family Genogram to identify dysfunctional behaviors and events that cause emotional and mental health problems such as abuse, abandonment, addictions, deaths, and health-related issues.

In the God-Realization Genogram, we rename dysfunctional family patterns to trace our negative love bonds back to our family's fall from grace and the Ten Spiritual Keys. To identify the patterns that have led us astray, like sheep lost in the woods, we can trace the consequences that we, our parents, and our ancestors experienced from the fall from grace. For our personal growth and understanding, we have worked with each Spiritual Key and its relationship to my husband's and my personal healing journeys. It has been important to contemplate the meaning of each key on our hearts, souls, eyes, and hands, praying for truth and wisdom about how each relates to our family history and our reentry into the Garden of Eden, Divine oneness. Working with each key has helped us to master the forces of separation.

For understanding the God-Realization Genogram, we will focus on the shameful feelings arising when anyone in our family breaks or disregards any one of the Ten Spiritual Keys, and the underlying transference of their pain and shame into the conscious and unconscious energy field of the whole family—the *mind field* that holds all of our family experiences, beliefs, and emotions, and that passes on to and affects each descendant. Uncovering and healing the shame in the family is one of the ways we can re-enter the garden, once again becoming comfortably naked, undefended, and at-one with God.

I first started using the term *God-Realization* in reference to creating the God-Realization Genogram. After reading Scripture and tracing the spiritual journey of the family, I was always led back into the Garden of Eden and spiritual oneness with our Creator; this is what I call God-Realization. It seems that each individual is on the path of self-realization, reaching their potential, and eventually will move into a state of God-Realization, where living from knowing that we are all part of the holy oneness of our Creator is the ultimate goal.

In this book, we will trace our family history back to the Garden of Eden, unraveling the greater mystery of God-Realization while we restore, heal, or unwind any crooked paths or negative love bonds (NLB) that inhibit our light or Divinity from full expression and radiance. In this process, we are learning a sense of self-mastery that leads us from self-actualization into God-Realization. This is the main path of humanity: to become God-Realized, born again, and at one with each other. Knowing this truth brings true peace and harmony to the world.

In order to do so, we will need to create our Family Genogram and trace anything that might inhibit God-Realization in the family. The Ten Spiritual Keys (Ten Commandments) will be used to identify how we lost our way. These Keys are a gift from God to our true awakening. We are fortunate that through both Moses and Christ, God offers us the opportunity to unravel the mystery and master the unbridled serpent within (our impulsiveness). By looking at the patterns in the family and seeing how they relate to breaking the spiritual laws hidden within the mystery of the Ten Commandments, we have the secret Keys toward self-mastery and God-Realization.

For example, in both my and my husband's families, there were several adulterous affairs. I was born into the seeds of adultery, hidden secrets, betrayal, scapegoating, and lies. If I stayed focused on the negative aspects of these acts, I would never find my true Divine potential. In the same way, my husband knew of adultery in his family, by his father and maternal grandfather. Both of us come to our relationship with a history that needs some exploring and healing. Both stories reflect the human struggles of our families' and ancestors' fall from grace and their search for the light within them. If my husband and I only focused on the adultery, we could become blinded to a much bigger picture where true forgiveness, mercy, and understanding reside. This is what Christ was teaching us when he instructed Peter to forgive seventy times seven.

Practicing forgiveness requires us to open our *cone of perception*, our awareness, to the different situations our relatives faced prior to losing faith. It also identifies patterns that may have gone on for several generations, where other Commandments or Spiritual Keys were forgotten or misunderstood. These complex relationships require us to forgive many people within our ancestral tree, to restore the blessings of a thousand generations. So it isn't too farfetched to say we need to forgive seventy times seven. Our return to embodying the Ten Spiritual Keys will help us with self-mastery and God-Realization. Our reentry into the Garden of Eden will be without shame. We can become naked again, undefended before our Creator, and rest in the bosom of oneness.

Using the God-Realization Genogram

Our natural Divine nature is lost to illusory layers of personal, familial, and social distortions. The restoration of one's true nature can be achieved by tracing the family challenges for insight, clarity, and healing. Each religion offers spiritual truths that bring wholeness to the individual and the family.

I am proposing expanding the knowledge of the Family Genogram to the God-Realization Genogram (GRG). For me, becoming God-Realized challenges us to move beyond self-realization to God-Realization. The GRG allows us to trace each of our negative and positive love bonds (PLB) to a breach in one of the Spiritual Keys and the teachings of Moses and Jesus. It also affords us opportunities to use biblical truths, prayers, and healing to release negative patterns and restore our Divine nature. Prayer, meditation, and self-evaluation were part of our ancestors' spiritual responsibility to God, the family, society, and the world. Returning to the holistic nature of these spiritual truths can restore health to us, to our families, and to the community as a whole.

As you examine your GRG, you'll continually be challenged to change your *cone of perception*, the habitual way you tend to look at the world, based on unresolved past conflicts or emotional and mental colorings you experienced during your developmental years. Some of these perceptions need to be challenged if you are to grow, expand your awareness, and be freed from the negative love bonds that are transferred onto others. You might discover, for instance, that something you thought your parents did out of anger or punishment was, in fact, motivated by love and a desire to protect you. The action itself can never change; it happened in the past, and what's done is done. However, the way in which you view the action and how you feel about it is always open and available for change. That is where you'll begin your healing.

Through the GRG, you will also connect your discoveries to the families of the Bible and explore their greatest lessons. Biblical stories unveil deep, profound teachings on the complexities of family relationships, while offering us the keys to explore our spiritual heritage and atonement with God, our Divine Creator. Biblical stories reveal the internal and external spiritual struggles families endured as they evolved on the planet over thousands of years. The stories highlight our genealogical past and illustrate both the positive and negative consequences of actions passed down generationally. By tracing the origins of both positive and negative familial patterns, we become aware of the intrinsic nature of the link between our present behavior and our ancestral heritage. This knowledge empowers us to make changes in our current life. Throughout the pages of the both the Old and New Testaments, we are given simple instructions to open up to blessings and communication with our Divine Creator. We are not doomed by our ancestral pasts; we have the power to change the here and now by living and expressing the greatest teachings ever written.

Traditional and God-Realization Genogram (GRG) Symbols

In order to create your own GRG, you will need to learn some basic symbols. These symbols are used in family therapy to identify relationships between people. I have included a graph of symbols here, and you can also find them on my website (www.livingfromgrace.com) for reference in creating your own GRG. When we can identify both positive and negative patterns in our family, we become empowered. This book doesn't replace working with a seasoned family therapist; rather, it is a tool to inspire you to identify your spiritual journey that goes beyond a traditional family therapy model. It includes the spiritual journey of your family, based on their direct relationship with God, and uses the Ten Spiritual Keys as a guide toward wholeness and holiness. This is a faith-based approach to family systems healing. You may not ascribe to Judaic-Christian philosophy, and if you do not, I encourage you to insert ten wisdom truths from your own spiritual practices. I believe you will uncover some of the same teachings and find the light within your family.

Standard Genogram Symbols

There are standard Genogram symbols that help classify gender, age, marriage, death, physical and mental health problems, and other basic information. See the Genogram symbol chart. These symbols will help you create your own genogram.

Standard Genogram Relationship Symbols

Relationships between people are complex. These complexities can be charted by using some of the following symbols. The symbols help you identify patterns of a healthy relationship between people and other issues that may signify a negative love bond pattern, such as divorce, living arrangements, estrangement, abuse, abandonment, adoptions, and isolation, and so on. Locate the symbols that best represent the relationships between people. Use the chart below to help simplify the process.

Family Genogram Symbols

☐	Male	⊠	Male (deceased)
○	Female	⊘	Female (deceased)
◇	Pet	◈	Pet (deceased)
?	Unknown (Stillbirth, Miscarriage, Transgender)	⸮	Unknown (deceased)

Child Link and Special Birth Symbols

Biological Child · Adopted Child · Foster Child · Pregnancy · Miscarriage · Abortion · Male Stillbirth · Female Stillbirth

Family / Emotional Relationships

Marriage	Separation in fact
Legal Separation	Divorce
Widowed	Cohabitation
Rape / Forced Relationship	Cut off / Estranged
Indifferent /Apathetic	Distant / Poor
Friendship / Close	Intimacy / Very Close
Hostile / Conflictual	Violence
Physical Abuse	Emotional Abuse
Sexual Abuse	Neglect (abuse)

You Shall Have No Other Gods Before Me

Key 1

You Shall Have No Graven Images

Key 2

You Shall Not Use The Lord's Name in Vain

Key 3

You Shall Keep The Sabbath Holy

Key 4

You Shall Honor Thy Mother and Father

Key 5

You Shall Not Commit Adultery

Key 6

You Shall Not Kill

Key 7

You Shall Not Steal

Key 8

You Shall Not Bear False Witness

Key 9

You Shall Not Covet

Key 10

God-Realization Genogram: The Ten Spiritual Keys Chart

This Ten Spiritual Keys chart is used as a guide to track different negative love bonds (NLB) in your family with the breaches in one of the Keys. The Keys are used to open your heart, soul, eyes, and hands to the light within. They will help you master any of the negative forces caused by your human struggles. You will track positive and negative generational love bonds, both paternal and maternal, in order to identify keys that might help you restore your relationship with God. The Keys help you stay focused on the main goal of God-Realization, rather than finger-pointing with blame, guilt, or shame. You are looking for clues to the spiritual journey of your family.

Once you identify the different NLB patterns in your family, contemplate which of the Ten Spiritual Keys were possibly broken. For example, in both my paternal and maternal family tree, we can identify significant patterns of adultery, extreme cutting off of family members, and internal and external family adoptions. Each of these patterns set up different negative love bonds within the descendants where, consciously or unconsciously, descendants have acted out one or more of these behaviors. In my family, several of the Commandments were disregarded, causing an influx of other related problems. For example, both paternal and maternal family members ostracized others or their descendants because of adultery or marrying outside of the family culture or lineage, possibly even because of greed over inheritance rights. In my Family Tree of Knowledge, all of the Ten Commandments were broken and the fall from grace was inevitable. When you look at your family struggles from the place of your Divine heritage, you can see how your light may be "covered under a bushel," as Christ described.

Until I was guided to write this book, I had never considered how the Ten Spiritual Keys were essential to my gaining entry into the Garden of Eden and transforming the family mind field (which many times felt like a mine field) that I was born into. Once you use the Spiritual Keys to identify how your relationship with God can be blocked, you will be surprised how easy it is for you to work towards restoration and healing. Each key offers you an opportunity to open to the light within and master the unbridled serpent energy that was a gift from our Creator. You are the one who will be faced with both the blessings and consequences of your actions, as well as those of your ancestors.

I will use my own family example to illustrate how you can use the God-Realization Genogram to help restore the light within you, your family, and your community. Usually in our families, there are several people with different types of relationships or issues. For me, it was important to focus on only a few at first to avoid feeling overwhelmed or confused. The few I chose to highlight on my spiritual journey were adoption, estrangement-scapegoating, adultery, and mental health issues. Later in the book, you will explore how complex these issues can become as you untangle the web and move toward the light within you.

You'll see that both my maternal and paternal genograms reveal valuable information for my spiritual journey and the main soul growth issues I faced growing up. You can use my example to help you start your own genogram. You may want to create one main diagram for your mother's family and another for your father's. If you are adopted and have information about your biological family, you can include it on a separate genogram. Keep all your genograms for referencing your spiritual journey as a family. Remember, you are reclassifying these patterns as positive and negative love bonds and reserving the term dysfunctional to describe only the most critical situations, where family members are severely impaired and are not thriving.

After you have created each genogram, using as much information you can, it is important to place both parents' genograms on the same page to compare what soul growth patterns and positive and negative love bonds mirror each other and point to the spiritual growth of the family. It can be frustrating at first trying to chart everything, but have fun with this process! Remember, your family tree goes back to the beginning, and looking at the present patterns can feel complex. You can use the examples here or download charts and instructions from my webpage, www.livingfromgrace.com, to help you with your GRG. You can also refer to the companion workbook, as it will help you and your partner work toward God-Realization together.

Maternal Genogram Chart

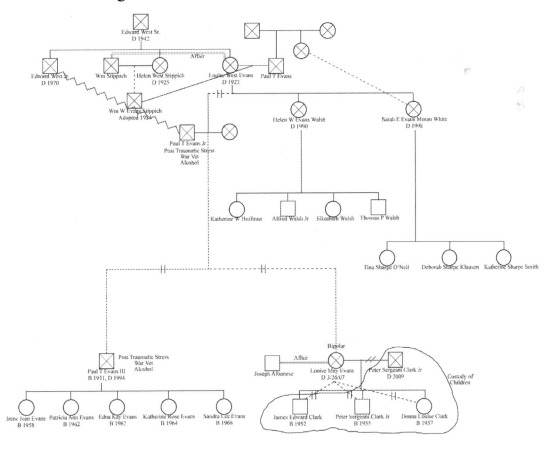

Paternal Chart

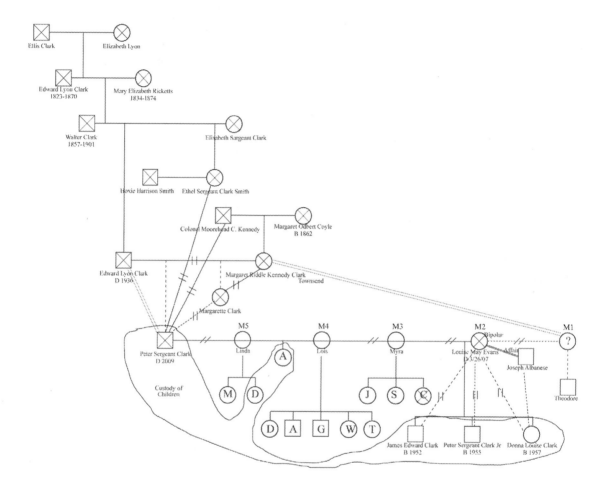

Start by graphing your relatives on a chart for up to four generations. Next, identify two or three positive (PLB) or negative love bonds (NLB). Sometimes we lose sight of the positive and focus only on the negative. The positive signifies that you are functioning today in healthy, positive ways. Only certain thoughts, actions, or emotions are stuck in the negative love bonds. In the GRG, you need to identify the positive to help you transform the negative. You may be overwhelmed by your circumstances and feel stuck in the pit of despair or negative thinking. If this happens, find a family member, a close friend, your pastor, a Living from Grace practitioner, or a competent therapist to help you identify your positive qualities. They may help you to identify your blind spots. This is why the God-Realization Genogram is important: It helps you take everything that is held inside you and place it outside on the chart. You can then see and understand how to restore your life and reclaim your Divine heritage.

Looking at my Family Tree of Knowledge, most people would label us as dysfunctional. Nevertheless, I choose another way to see the struggles and hardships of my family—as a journey toward God-Realization, on the way to heal ourselves, our family, and future generations. We can identify the negative love bonds, take responsibility for the consequences, transform and restore our Divine qualities, and open to the blessings of a thousand generations. This is God's promise!

My Family Tree of Knowledge

When you view each chart, you will immediately notice how both my mother and father were cut off or estranged from their parents and relatives. These types of situations can be confusing for the children of the parent who is cut off. Just as we did, these children grow up missing out on the richness of grandparents, aunts, uncles, cousins, and their heritage. It is like they are born into a family secret, a blind spot that longs for insight and healing. In addition to negative love bonds forming around secrets and to being the outcasts, adultery, adoption, and divorce are three other major themes in both of my parental charts. This is what I learned in my family. It was the family mind field I was born into. Many of you looking at these charts might immediately think, "What a dysfunctional family!" or "How unfortunate for those kids." You might start to blame or make preliminary assumptions and judgments. I ask you to expand your perception to exploring the spiritual journey hidden beneath the unhealthy behavior and actions. This is where you will uncover and see the grace and light that resides in all families, regardless of their fall from grace.

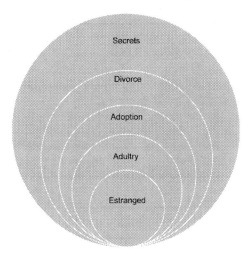

Charting the patterns, beliefs, or emotions on a concentric circle chart offers a visual representation of the types of situations you were born into. The circle chart helps you to identify emotions, beliefs, and family patterns that can lead you to the restoration process. It is a positive way to move toward attaining self-mastery and reclaiming the light in your family.

Another way to look at the mind field of the family is to see how it floats around you at birth. When you review my chart, you will see that my Divine essence was born into this invisible family mind field. All of these conscious and unconscious situations are available and are imprinted within us. Yet, newborns or young children cannot verbally communicate the impressions, feelings, and thoughts they are experiencing at birth. It is only when we reflect on our Family Tree of Knowledge that we can truly understand our negative love bonds, release them, and reclaim the light within us.

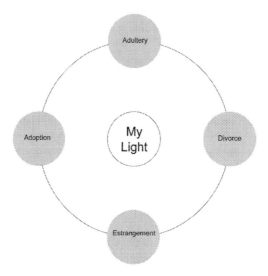

There are also positive love bonds that formed as a result of the hardships. It is important for you to identify these too! Most of us can hold onto the negative and become blinded to the positive. The adoptions in the family provided essential Divine qualities for creating positive love bonds. I can identify that out of hardship and pain, I acquired security, love, respect, and an adventurous nature. These positive qualities helped to shape most of my personality. The negative love bonds created areas in my life where I struggle to reclaim the light within and to release the thoughts, feelings, and actions that support them. By identifying the innate and reinforced positive qualities, I can use them to change the negative.

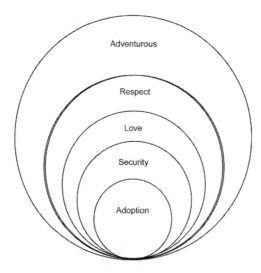

My Maternal Ancestral Chart- Four Generations

Sometimes money and entitlement can separate for generations. I have outlined four generations of my mother's chart and included as much as I know. Some of the relatives are still alive, yet because of Edward West Sr.'s Will and Trust, a family split continued over many years. Secrets can be passed on for several generations, so the truth is clouded over by everyone's limited cone of perception. In my maternal chart, there are hidden stories surrounding the adultery of my great-great grandmother, Louise West Evans with her brother-in-law, William Stippach. This story was to be a hidden secret, yet as the mind field of the family holds all of this information, my mother, Louise Mae Evans, committed adultery herself. In both of these situations, an adoption took place. Upon the death of my great-great grandmother Louise, her sister and brother-in-law adopted her son. My mother and her husband Peter (my non-biological father) took me. Peter's name was on the birth certificate, and no one stopped him. The adoptions were positive love bonds for the children, even though negative love bonds were created between relatives. These negative love bonds included being cut off and estranged from other family members.

My Paternal Ancestral Chart – Four Generations

In my father's chart, I have also outlined four generations. These were hard to trace since my father was cut off and estranged from his adoptive family after he left his first wife and married my mother. The story of this estrangement was a family secret that my father took to his grave. Some of the information provided here comes from one of my father's files, my Internet research, and a few stories. From what my mother and a little of what my father told me, my father was married before my mother. He had a son named Theodore. Something happened that broke the marriage up, though there are differing versions of the story, one claiming it was my father's adultery, and the other claiming it was his wife's love for her high school sweetheart. Regardless of the reason, it was a big deal back in the fifties since wealthy families tended to arrange marriages. When he was thirteen, my father had gone through a major ordeal of acting out after his father passed away. He went to private schools and military school, just like his grandfather. His great-great grandfather, Colonel Moorhead C. Kennedy, was a prominent businessman in Philadelphia.

In my paternal genogram, you will recognize some of the same patterns of adoption, estrangement and being cut off from the family, and adultery. My father's chart shows how he repeated the same negative love bond with his mother in four other marriages, where he assumed custody of his children and also of one of my step-sisters. My father repeated this pattern unconsciously as he was trying to heal this deep wound and scar. I often wonder if this, too, may go back to his biological parents and the patterns in their family.

Application of GRG Keys to Both Charts

You will notice that in both families, my brothers, sister, and I were born into secrets, extramarital affairs, estrangement, and adoption patterns. Some of these created positive love bonds while others created negative ones. You may see how adultery caused estrangement from certain family members yet built strength in the person who was cut off. Or, you may see how adultery affected the children of the adulterer in either positive or negative ways. Another example of complexity is that in both sides of my family, both positive and negative love bonds formed around adoptions. These love bonds illustrate how a baby or child can adapt to unconscious mind field of his/her Family Tree of Knowledge. Without knowledge of these love bonds we can repeat the same patterns, often for generations. Let's explore how.

For the West Family, adoption was a necessity after Louise West Evans I died. The family pulled together after a tragedy to help Paul Evans I take care of four children. There was stipulation in Great-Great Grandfather West's Will that his son Edward could not adopt outside of the family and that family money would stay in the family. This set up a negative love bond between my grandfather, Paul Evans II, and Edward West Jr. If Edward didn't have an heir, the final distribution of the monies would go to my uncle and mother, the last living descendants before my GG Grandfather West died.

In my father's family, both he and his sister were adopted, which led to certain outcomes. His first son was adopted by his ex-wife's new husband, and he secretly adopted me by keeping his name on my birth certificate, even after finding out about my mother's affair. Both my brother Pete and I adopted our spouse's children, so the pattern continued. You may think, "Wow! What a family story! How could anyone learn to trust, love, and respect God, seeing all of these complexities and negative love bonds?"

When you expand your cone of perception, you can see how each negative situation can relate to breaking several of the Ten Commandments. In my chart, many of my paternal and maternal family members breached several of the Commandments. All of them were broken at one point or another. The behaviors, actions, and words of my relatives were like a cloud hovering over our family. In my diagrams, you can witness how the crooked paths of our ancestors and parents covered our light.

The way toward restoring the Family Tree of Knowledge would be to contemplate each Commandment, restore the light within my heart, soul, eyes, and hands, and to embrace, love, and forgive others. I would need to pray and meditate for deeper truth and surrender my limited perceptions and pain to open to the greater mystery. The process is one of freedom. Just as the Jewish people were freed from bondage, you can become free from the bondage of your generational negative love bonds. The Ten Spiritual Keys were given to open our direct communication with God and restore the people to wholeness and holiness. You can use those very same keys to restore your family. Remember that the Jewish people were too afraid to venture up the mountain with Moses, and they stayed behind and waited. While waiting, they became afraid. I invite you to climb the mountain, to look at your family in a new way, and to meditate on each of the Ten Commandments in order to see clearly.

God presses us forward in our quest to find our way back into the light. The road may not be an easy one, yet one lesson I've learned is that God is always seeking us out, regardless of the stories we were born into. The light within us is pressing us forward to unwind the past and restore our

Divine nature. I found this to be true over and over as I was guided to read the Bible and explore my ancestral tree. Again, I invite you to climb the mountain with Moses. You will be rewarded, I promise! If proof is what you need, look back at some of the blessings that were hidden within my family.

I discovered that in 1864, my Great-Great-Great Grandfather, Edward Lyon Clark I, was the warden of the Christ Church in Philadelphia. Throughout my adult life, I have felt a presence guiding me, blessing me, encouraging me to uncover and tell these stories, reclaim my ancestral history, and restore my family to wholeness. I have felt both the blessings and consequences of both my maternal and paternal families. Yet, I feel the richness of blessing in what I once thought of as a curse. The estrangement my father experienced motivated him to take custody of all of his children, even me. My heart is filled with his unconditional love that will sustain me for eternity. Money could never replace the love and gratitude I have for my father. So, in one branch of the tree, there is a negative love bond being created, while in another branch a positive love bond is born. Just as my great-great-great grandfather was a record keeper, one who preserves history, I, too, yearn to tell and reclaim the history of my heritage. I think he would approve of keeping the historical records of our Family Tree of Knowledge intact.

When we expand our perceptions and learn more about our ancestral tree, we can open ourselves to know the truth, restore our light, and heal our family. If we continue to see these patterns as dysfunctional, we may never become God-Realized and find our way back home. I found that out of each crooked path, both positive and negative love bonds form. I also found that we are guided by our ancestors. Some will be blessings to us, while others are waiting for us to unravel the mystery of the crooked path. Regardless of the situations and circumstances of your birth and your ancestral heritage, you are called by God to restore your relationship and heal your life and family.

You may need to meditate and work with several of the Keys to clear your direct communication with God and transform your ancestral heritage. Just as Christ went to the desert for forty days to master His internal struggle between the voice of God and the voice of the tempter, you may need to do the same. Because of our heritage, we have many negative voices inside that need to be tamed while we restore the Divine qualities within. You have to power to restore yourself!

How to Create Your Own GRG

Creating your own God-Realization Genogram (GRG) can illuminate your spiritual journey and give you insight and tools for living a healthy, spiritual, and fruitful life.

Start by making your Family Genogram Chart(s), using the following information:

1. Answer basic family history questions about parents, children, grandparents, aunts, and uncles.
2. Fill out the relationship forms to help you identify these patterns.
3. Chart the relationship issues between people on a genogram.

4. Identify and trace psychological illnesses and their effects. These include depression, alcoholism, post-traumatic stress, and so on. The effects might include adultery, divorce, adoption, and war, just to name a few.

5. Identify and trace medical histories. This includes heart disease, diabetes, mental health challenges, dementia, miscarriages, and so on. Family effects may include hospitalizations, family crisis interventions, anxiety, anger, or depression in caregivers or siblings.

6. Identify both positive and negative beliefs that are held within the family and that support positive or negative generational love bonds. For example, one person who was abandoned may believe, "Nobody cares or loves me," while another person may form the belief, "I don't need anyone. People can't be trusted." What are some of the beliefs in your family? You can chart both the healthy ones and unhealthy ones.

7. Identify emotional colorings. Emotions are basically 'yum' or 'yuck'. They further refine to anger, sadness, fear, shame, and joy. Choose one or two to focus on in the beginning.

8. Identify major fears, like fear of people in general or fear of institutions (trust issues) or rigidity (fear of losing control), to name just a couple.

9. Next, look at where people disconnected from their spiritual connection. Were there people who lost their inheritance?

10. How do these negative love bonds relate to the Ten Spiritual Keys?

11. You can find samples of these charts in the *Blessings From A Thousand Generations Companion Workbook.*

In Chapter 4 and in Part 2, you will explore how to work with each of the Ten Commandments (Spiritual Keys) to restore your heart, soul, eyes, and hands and to master generational negative love bonds, receive the blessings of a thousand generations, and restore your relationship with God. These Keys will help you heal yourself, your family, and those around you.

Chapter 4

The Ten Spiritual Keys

Know therefore that the Lord your God is God; he is the faithful God, keeping his covenant of love to a thousand generations of those who love him and keep his commands. ~Deuteronomy 7:9

Why did Moses go to the top of Mount Sinai? Unfortunately, after forced enslavement for several generations, the Jewish people had lost their connection to God and adopted many Egyptian customs. Their moral code and behavior had deteriorated. They were living in despair and a profound forgetfulness of their ancestral heritage and their roots in Divine oneness. Moses was deeply concerned for his people when he ascended to the top of Mount Sinai to meditate and reflect on God's guidance. Delivering them from Egypt, it turned out, had been only the first step. Now they were complaining and afraid, questioning Moses for leading them into the wilderness without a plan. They wondered how he would help his people reclaim their birthright and restore order and peace, how he would lead them into the Promised Land.

During his forty days and nights on Mount Sinai, Moses must have asked, "What's wrong with my people? How did we lose our way?" He must have reflected on his ancestral heritage and all the stories he knew for clues, guidance, and insights. And he must have reflected on his own and his ancestors' broken relationship with God and the consequences that had followed.

In the story of Moses, we are reminded of these fundamental truths, and like Moses, we are given the Ten Commandments as specific Keys to enlightenment and God-Realization. Through his adoption, loss of identity, finding his true self, rediscovering and listening to God's directions and Commandments, and fulfilling his destiny, Moses' story can guide those of us who have lost our way with similar family or social problems. Moses is a significant leader who can offer us hope, keys to a deeper understanding of our spiritual journey, and opportunities to heal our ancestral heritage.

To begin your spiritual journey, you too, will have to go to the mountaintop, just like Moses. When you're in your life, in the very center of it, you only see the maelstrom. You have to get outside of yourself and reflect on where you've been and what you want to become. This is a process of self-mastery. How do you become illuminated in your body, your soul, your eyes, and your hands? How do you master the life force that has been given to you? How do you reflect this to your partner, your children, and your community?

You can start by using the Spiritual Keys to open your direct relationship with God. When you meditate and pray with each Key on your heart, soul, eyes, and hands, the sacred light within you radiates forth into your life. You become like Moses on the mountaintop: observing your life, reclaiming your Divine heritage, and transforming your negative love bonds. You can achieve self-mastery and tame your unbridled desires when you are in direct relationship with God. Your authentic power and radiance can now be shared with your partner, children, and your community.

You may not realize it, but I'm willing to guess you've already been seeking the wisdom hidden within these Keys for a long time. How do I know? Because we buy hundreds of self-help books that give us seven, ten, or maybe fifteen rules for self-improvement, financial success, and living a better life. We hunger for books that revise, change, and massage these biblical teachings and other spiritual truths into a palpable language for the general public. We are constantly seeking, contemplating, meditating on truth—and still miss the ten basic Keys to the Garden of Eden and living a God-Realized life. Maybe you've felt the Keys are no longer relevant in our modern-day world. Maybe you've felt they aren't relevant to your life, to your everyday struggles.

Right here, right now, I invite you to review the Ten Commandments, the Spiritual Keys, with fresh eyes. Moses went to the mountaintop and pondered many of the same questions you are struggling with today for your family: "What's wrong? How did we lose our way?" He returned with the Ten Commandments as his answer. And if you review them with new eyes, you'll see they can be your answer as well.

If you are skeptical about the Keys or if you still feel uncomfortable thinking about the Ten Commandments, you can use the Bible's Ten Beatitudes or any other keys from your spiritual tradition. You can also reframe a Commandment in the form of a positive affirmation to help you embrace and experience its true meaning. The first three Commandments, for instance, sound more like demands than an invitation to understand the exquisite nature of our Beloved Creator. But if you reframe them, they become:

Positive Affirmation, First Commandment
I honor one God, the eternal creative force of the universe.

Positive Affirmation, Second Commandment
I surrender all attachments to the material world and know only one God.

Positive Affirmation, Third Commandment
I surrender my ego, pride, and vanity and know God.

Really, it is okay to do this! You are not changing the meaning of the Commandments. You are opening yourself to a deeper understanding with words that resonate with you. The main purpose of the Covenant was not to become stuck on words like laws, to lord over people. It was to enhance your direct relationship with God, to open your heart, soul, eyes, and hands, and to illuminate the light with your partner, children, and community.

Bonding with God's Word

Therefore shall ye lay up these my words in your heart and in your soul, and bind them for a sign upon your hand, that they may be as frontlets between your eyes. And ye shall teach them to you children, speaking of them when thou sittest in thine house, and when thou walkest by the way, when thou liest down, and when thou risest up. And thou shalt write them upon the door posts of thine house, and upon thy gates. ~Deuteronomy 11:18-20 (King James Version)

In the rest of this section we will, chapter-by-chapter, review each of the Ten Spiritual Keys with this Deuteronomy reference in mind. It tells us that, first and foremost, we need to embody the Ten Commandments for purification and atonement with God. Living in union with God, our moral code becomes the very fabric of our lives. In essence, when we embody the Ten Commandments, all of life is blessed, and we are always standing on holy ground. This sacred teaching can restore peace and order within us, our families, our work, our community, and the world. You'll learn how to embody the Keys, just as Deuteronomy describes, so that you, like Moses, can open your way to communication with God by:

Purifying Your Heart

Purifying Your Soul

Purifying Your Hands

Purifying Your Eyes

Teaching your Children

Purifying and Protecting Your House

Purifying Your Heart

Praying and meditating on each Spiritual Key opens the doorways to the heart and purifies any unresolved conflicts that prevent us from loving ourselves and others. Each Key holds the secret to sacred communion with God. It provides us with the opportunity to cleanse and purify any crooked way that results in unresolved beliefs, feelings of blame, jealousy, judgments, resentments, and hatred. These negative recycled beliefs and emotions block us from receiving and giving love and, when left unhealed, can be the source of generations of pain and suffering.

You'll begin this purification process by contemplating what is in your heart at this very moment. Do you have anything in your heart other than attention to the Divine? We all have many things in our hearts, but what holds your focus? What comes first? Your actions will leave many clues to the answer. Do you behave in such a way that says your car, for instance, is more important than your child? Maybe you've overreacted when your child spilled a drink on the seat or your teenager accidentally scratched the paint in a parking garage. Maybe you've had an accident and you were—deep down—more concerned with what happened to the car than whether the people inside it were okay.

Are you so caught up in one of your life problems that it has displaced God and become, in a sense, your idol? My father always called this, "making a mountain out of a molehill," and I've seen it happen so many times. A person will come to me for healing and actually resist the process of healing because they are more rooted in their story than in the Divine. The story has become their big thing. They keep playing that scratch in the record again and again because they really don't know who they would be if they finally solved the problem. They've idolized the story, and they become rooted in it. They orient themselves to the world from that story rather than centering in their Divine self. That's why some people feel empty even though they've done a lot of work and made a lot of accomplishments. They keep rooting into trying to prove themselves, or they have an idealized image of what they're supposed to be in the world, but when they achieve that, it's still not fulfilling them. Why is this? They may be looking at the wrong places for self-fulfillment. They think, "I get to the top of my job, and then what? Was that my only goal in life?"

Let's talk about one of the Keys, like making the Sabbath holy. With all the daily stress in our life, many of us don't have time to spend a whole day resting and contemplating our relationship with God. Some people are so busy it is even difficult to take a *Sabbath moment* during the day. I am sure many of us would love the luxury to spend forty days at the mountaintop like Moses to reflect on our life and our children. Yet, we can learn to take Sabbath moments throughout our day to reflect on our lives. People are so hungry today and want to meditate, pray and bring peace into their bodies, minds, and spirits.

You may also purify your heart by reflecting on the Key, *"Honor thy mother and father."* This may open you to all the love you received from them and feel like a refreshing bath of love. Or, perhaps you're carrying unresolved pain from your childhood and find it difficult to forgive your parents. Your heart may be twisted in knots and confused because of a parent who was cruel or harmful. These unresolved feelings can hold you hostage to the past and suppress all the love that is available to you. Exploring your Family Tree of Knowledge can offer you deeper insights into your parent's past, help you identity the negative love bonds, and eventually open you to receive the blessings from a thousand generations. You may uncover hidden secrets held within the family mind field that will inspire you to practice forgiveness seventy times seven. You will learn why Christ instructed us to forgive "seventy times seven." True forgiveness may release seventy times seven—or more—people in our ancestral tree.

Purifying Your Soul

We say things like, "She has a beautiful soul. He lost his soul. Lift this burden from my soul." We reference our soul as a living and breathing aspect of our consciousness. God wants us to purify our soul and claim the light within us. Your soul carries all the wisdom and knowledge of your spiritual journey and the Divine potential of your life. You're restoring your soul so you can release any negative love bonds that hold you hostage to the past and so you can fulfill your divine potential. When you remove any shrouds covering your soul, you are born again and again from a place of grace, light, and wisdom. If you strive to purify your soul, then when your soul leaves to join the spirit world, it will leave from a place of light, unencumbered by the generational negative love bonds and unresolved personal conflicts. For example, your unresolved negative love bonds hold you hostage to those same people in the spirit world until you surrender into the light and unravel the mystery of forgiveness and blessings.

Your life experiences—both positive and negative—cover your soul light and are written into the Book of Life, God's record. You are already in heaven from the Divine light within you, yet you're taking these unresolved aspects with you. Your light is covered by your unhealthy thoughts, feelings, doubts, or wrongdoings. You leave your earthly existence tied to unresolved issues. It is always good to clear these before the time of death. All of us who have fallen from grace are promised that through forgiveness of sins we are welcome in the Kingdom of God.

You're asking your soul the age-old questions: "What have I come for? What do I wish to create in the world?" Everyone was born with Divine potential. When you're contemplating your soul, you're contemplating your Divine potential in this lifetime. Is there something blocking your potential? Have you lost some of your dreams because you've lost your connection to Spirit? In her book, *Light Emerging: The Journey of Personal Healing*, Dr. Brennan talks about having a shroud over your soul seat (located above the heart area) that inhibits a person from fulfilling their purpose in life—like a dark cloud that resides over one's soul.

Each soul grows through different experiences or life lessons. Everyone has different life lessons to master. If you're born into a family that has been affected by adultery, maybe you're mastering that soul growth issue around adultery so you don't pass it down generationally. If there's been abuse in the family, there will be people struggling to heal these issues so they don't pass it down to the next generation. It's up to you to spend time contemplating what your soul's life lesson may be so you can free it to create what you were meant to create in this world. Maybe your Divine potential is to heal the very issues you were born into so you can bring light and understanding to others who may have suffered in the same way.

Purifying the Hands

In the purification of your hands, it helps to think of this: There is energy in your hands. It is the energy that honors the God within you, and when you touch others, you are ideally doing so from a place of honoring the God in you and in them. You can go even further: When you embody the Spiritual Keys in your hands, your hands will be less likely to act out against those Keys.

For instance, ponder the Key, *"You shall not steal."* If that is in your hands, you will not steal. *"You shall not murder."* If that's in your hands, you will not kill someone. *"You shall not commit adultery."* That means you will not put your hands on someone you shouldn't touch. We're supposed to be living these Keys. When we do so, we're honoring people and our heritage, and we're touching people from a place of grace.

The Keys keep our hands clean so they can illuminate Divine light and become an instrument of Divine grace, love, and creativity. When we're not coveting, our hands can create what Spirit wants us to create in the world. Our hands are in alignment with Divine flow. We can sow the seeds we're here to sow in the world instead of trying to take the seeds from someone else. We see a lot of this now with identity theft. These thieves are so creative that they can steal someone else's entire existence, their identity. Such individuals have the potential to create wonderful things in the world—things that would probably bring them more money than they're going to the trouble of stealing. But because they're using their light to beat the system and steal from others, they're taking their intellect and creativity and twisting it. They've lost their own sense of identity, their connection.

When our hands are filled with grace, we can touch others with love and grace and compassion. We don't touch the person because we idolize them, and we don't touch them in anger or hatred. With these keys in all our hands, all abuse in the world would stop. It's like having a stream of consciousness that's purely coming from the Divine and that reaches out to create and touch others in the world.

Our hands can rest too. What does that mean? It means we have time to contemplate what we're doing before we grab or reach for something else or act compulsively. Allowing our hands to rest gives us time to reflect on what we are creating with them. It allows us to reflect on each of the Keys for restoring the light within them.

Purifying the Eyes

To purify your eyes, imagine putting the Commandments at the center of your eyes. Look through your eyes and think, "Am I looking through the eyes of God? Am I connected to God within so I'm seeing with that connection, or am I looking at what's wrong with the world?" Our eyes tell us a lot about what we're looking at and how we're looking at it. Are we looking through our eyes with judgment? Are we looking at all the things we can acquire? Are we looking at the next thing, such as wanting to get a new car or something that's wrong with the house that we have to fix? We might even be looking at what we think our child should be achieving, and those types of things can become dreadfully big and important when we should be looking at different things through purified eyes.

We are all rushing around these days, and it's not uncommon to hear people say, "I don't have time to meditate." But we do have time to take a Sabbath moment to think, "How am I seeing this? Am I looking at it from being connected to the Divine within me or within them? If I'm having a problem with a friend or colleague, can I see that they have generational issues too?" Remember that you bring your history into the workplace and so do your colleagues, so they may sometimes treat you like they were treated in their own family. You must look beyond the thought, "They're driving me nuts, and I wish they would get fired" to, "I bring my own cast of characters when I come into a room and so does everybody else." Underneath those things you're reacting to, that person is still trying to connect with their spiritual life just as much as you are, and they have a right to exist and be there just as much as you do.

From this example, you can see that how we look through our eyes and what's cluttering our eyes becomes very important. We may have a very limited cone of perception. A fundamentalist Christian, for instance, may have a literal belief in something, and they may be so attached to that belief that they think anything beyond it is completely foolish and untrue. They may see and judge the world from that place until their cone of perception is challenged and they have to expand it to include something different—the reality of another person.

How many times have you said, when you learned something new, "I didn't quite see it that way!" It happens in any basic argument with your spouse. You really can't see the other's point of view because of the limited way you were viewing the other person's responses and reactions. I may see a certain thing going on with my husband, and maybe that's not what's going on at all. I see a look on his face or a certain behavior, and I respond to that rather than ask him about what's really going on. We project our own perceptions onto others and believe them to be true when in reality they can be untrue and very limiting.

Christ talked a lot about the eyes, about being blinded, and about helping the blind to see. Sometimes a blind person can see farther than someone with sight. If you're only looking through your own view, you don't have the ability to have empathy for the other person. Jesus was always clearing and healing the eyes to teach us how important this Commandment is in our life. If our eyes are blinded by generations of ignorance, they will need to be purified with the Keys.

Gratitude plays a part here as well. When you are connected in this way, you're thankful and in a state of gratitude for everything in front of you. If you're in a state of gratitude, it can take you to a place of letting go of some of your limiting points of view. When you look at situations through the eyes of the Divine, you become truly grateful for what is. Those disappointments, misconceptions, and unresolved feelings surrender into a deeper truth. You may have awakened another aspect of your light, love, compassion, and forgiveness. And for this you can be truly grateful.

Placing the Ten Spiritual Keys on the frontlet of our eyes is the way God has instructed us in the purification process. God wants us to see the light in ourselves and in others. We were given these Commandments to open us to the light within and see the truth. When we purify our eyes, our vision expands to include a myriad of perceptual realities and to see the universal truth of humanity. The process also helps us to visualize what we want to create in the world and bring it into fruition. Moreover, we can see hope and hopelessness side by side without losing our connection to seeing the Divine truth within a situation. Both hope and hopelessness become meaningless when you see God in everyone and everything.

Protection and Transmission to Your Children

We teach our children everything else they need to be well and make their way in the world. We teach them how to eat well and dress themselves, and we tell them when to go to school every day. If we do all this for them, it only makes sense that we need to teach them how to live and embody the Ten Spiritual Keys. Embodying the Keys in our lives and communing with God will provide the very seeds of purification that our children need to be born into—to be born without the burdens hidden within the Family Tree of Knowledge. When we teach these Keys to our children, it reaffirms their connection with God and offers them the opportunity to live a spiritual life. It also offers children a sense of internal peace they can rely on during times of stress, such as when a relative dies or family members are enduring a crisis.

While these are important reasons to instill the Keys in our children, one of the most important may be that the Keys can act as a kind of spiritual barrier, protecting children against the negativity of others. This negativity, in a child's world, often takes the forms of peer pressure and bullying. If a child has a poorly developed sense of self, s/he is vulnerable to the attacks, influences, and suggestions of others. However, knowing and practicing the Spiritual Keys will provide the foundation for our children's self-esteem and their sense of identity in the world. Without receiving these teachings, our children can become lost and led astray by other forces. With the teachings, our children learn empathy, love, and respect, and they will be armed with tools to master their impulses and make difficult choices. The Keys will give them a kind of moral compass they can consult. The Ten Keys provide a seal of inner and outer protection for us and our children, allowing for immanent grace to flow from within us and securing our atonement with the Divine Creator. They also allow for blessings to flow forward from our purification process so that light can radiate from us to our children and future generations.

The best way to teach the Commandments to our children is to allow them to see an example of living by them. You will always be your child's first and best role model. The moral code of ethics needs to be close to our hearts, to keep our connection with God and generationally transmit the importance of the connection. To be sure you are transmitting the right teachings and lessons, you can and should talk to your children about why you made a certain decision or how you think in a compassionate way toward a family member or a coworker.

Spiritually, our children can suffer if they don't understand these basic principles or other similar religious and spiritual principles within their culture. Intimate knowledge of the Ten Commandments as spiritual truths will protect our children's inner relationship with God and the blessings that come from that relationship. Allowing our children to walk in today's world without these principles is like sending them out into the cold naked, without anything to protect them. Without the Keys, children will have no spiritual understanding and will not be able to unify the world. If you think about it, each of these Keys resides naturally, deep within your child's subconscious, interwoven within the very fabric of their being. It is your job to activate the light within them, helping them to remember how to reestablish their relationship with God, who dwells within.

Protecting Your Home

Many Jewish families practice this by placing a *mezuzah*—a small, sacred container that encases a slip of paper with the Commandments written on it—on their doors. They face it toward the people walking in. Some people put it out on the fence or in the doorway to their living room. The idea is that the mezuzah is filled with the power of the spoken word written within, expressing "This is a house that honors these Commandments," and this house is spiritually protected. Symbolically, you may already have something hanging in or on your house. You might have a picture of Christ or a cross on the wall or some other symbol that announces your spiritual connection and the principles you live by.

Contemplate this: When someone walks into your house, do they feel that presence? Do they feel welcome when they're walking through the doorway? Do they feel your home is protected from thieves and danger? Is there energy in your home that says, "God lives here within each of us and within our home. You're welcome here. There's respect in our home"? Many homes have that feeling, and you can sense it, even if the owners haven't put words to it. You recognize it when you go into someone's home and you feel comfortable, safe, and secure. You feel the light in the home. You can put your pocketbook down and know no one's going to get into it. On the contrary, there are homes where you put your purse right behind your legs because you feel paranoid, not knowing if one of the kids or someone else might steal something from you. I've had that happen.

Even more than that, because the Scriptures have been passed down for thousands of years, the power of the written word has a kind of alchemical consciousness to it—a transfer of energy. When the house is filled with that kind of energy and something is out of alignment, you know almost right away. Sometimes you'll notice it if you have older kids and teen visitors start to come into the house. You might see one of your kid's friends and notice something sneaky or off with that new acquaintance. When you're in tune like this, you'll pick up on it very quickly; you'll know that something doesn't resonate inside of you, and you learn to listen to these subtle impressions. Something doesn't feel right, is not in alignment with what you, your family, or your house wants to be in alignment with.

When you are in tune, it wakes you up to many different things. You will know if a kid is doing drugs; you will simply pick up on it, sense it. But don't instantly assume you have a bad kid on your hands. It could be a lost kid who needs somebody to reach out to them, so don't be too quick to reject the child on the premise that you don't allow "that kind" in your home. This child may need extra attention, help, parental contemplation, or even intercessory prayer. Many times, I've prayed for kids without them knowing. I've met children whom I've felt were never prayed for, and they were so lost. When I meet such a child, there's so much pain in my heart knowing they are so very lost. I understand that most likely, the last four or five generations of their family tree lost their way and forgot how to pray for their children. So I pray for that child, asking God to protect them and keep them safe, to surround them with love and light. I ask for their healing and the spiritual restoration of their heart, soul, eyes, and hands. I surrender and ask on their behalf that God will work a miracle in their life. I ask that they find out the truth about the light within them. After the prayer, I let go and trust that God will find a way through the darkness. Can you do that? And, even better, can the child feel the presence of love and light in your home even as they walk over the threshold?

Consider now the potential of each of the Ten Keys to open the windows of light, love, and compassion within you. Can you see why God wants us to know and understand these wisdom truths? They are fundamental to living a God-Realized life and to our health and well-being. We have the secret to master the forces within and transmit our light to our partner, our family, our friends, our profession, and our world. We are born with the skills to master the negative love bonds and bring our Divine light forward. It is an inner process, and the Keys awaken that process within us. We can obtain this knowledge by going through the God-Realization Genogram process and committing to reclaim the light within us. The God-Realization experience raises awareness in all of those we touch. Give yourself the time to explore each of the Keys and their respective effects on your heart, soul, eyes, and hands. Notice how you transmit these to your family and activate them in your home. Enjoy your journey!

PART 2

THE TEN SPIRITUAL KEYS

Chapter 5

The First Commandment: The Key to Wholeness

You shall have no other Gods before me. ~ *Exodus 20:3*

The concept at the heart of this Commandment is truly wondrous. The Jewish people were taught to worship only one God when most of the known world, comprised of Egyptians, Greeks, and Romans, worshipped multiple deities. This mode of religion had worked for all these people for generations and, after all, isn't it better to have more than one of a good thing, especially a god? What threatened the Jews the most was becoming scattered and lost as a people. This First Commandment, as brought down by Moses, offered a tremendous solution: the gift of unity. It provided focus and purpose for the people, both as a community and as individuals.

The First Commandment is a message from God for all of us, to unify and understand universal oneness. It opens our mind-body connection to the depth of knowing God's true love for us and allows for the experience of direct communication with God. From Genesis, we learn that everything—earth, sky, planets, and universe—was formed from one life force. Humankind was created from the dust of the Earth, and our breath actually arises from the Divine within us. Our very nature, our cells as well as our breath, arise from this Universal Consciousness, which is God.

But in order to take in this knowledge, you'll have to examine—perhaps even challenge—how you see God. The First Commandment requires that each of us focus on our intimate relationship with God. Our beliefs about the nature of God play an important role in how we understand the First Commandment and what God is asking of us. Who is God in your life? Is God something or someone you pray to? Do you see Him as a long-bearded, white-haired man who answers prayers, or as a universal Presence inside of you? Even if you see the white-haired man, don't discount that image, for there is some truth in it for you. This is the image of the God you learned in your childhood or from church, and that image is based on different things. If you have immature beliefs and images about God left over from childhood, you need to observe how they affect you today. Are these images outdated or based on dogma and static thinking? Did you adapt the beliefs of your family or place of worship? Did you misinterpret what you were told, filtering the information from a child's perspective? Was God considered unobtainable or only accessible for some? Or you may be going outside of yourself to look for God.

But you must also consider the possibility of what Christ taught. According to His teachings, you are to meet God in the center of your heart. Christ says God and the Kingdom of God are within you. Expand your cone of perception to truly see and understand these concepts in your heart. The path you'll find through the Commandments will guide you. Your search is a spiritual journey, and everyone seeks their own understanding and truth about God. It is an active desire that runs throughout all humanity, the one thread that interconnects us. Examining your own journey and the journey of your ancestors offers you the opportunity to restore your relationship with God. Working with the First Commandment reestablishes your inner connection and roots you in this awareness. Our biblical ancestors might say that God needs to be your first order of business.

We access God through our consciousness by attuning our human mind and personal will to the mind and will of God. By directing your ego and will toward God-Realization, all types of awakening experiences can happen in your life. As you become more aware of that process, your desire to know God will be transmitted through the Universal Energy Consciousness. God is always listening and responding.

It's hard for our minds to grasp how God could be the activating principle in all of our consciousness. All of humanity's desires, hopes, dreams, and ideas have roots in Divine creativity. When we are in right relationship with God, our actions, words, and deeds make this world a better place to live. We use our free will and the power of our spoken word; the desires of our heart activate our Divine consciousness and transmit our thoughts and feelings universally. Our consciousness is always interacting with the Universal Consciousness. As new ideas emerge and we engage or disengage our personal will, our consciousness expands and contracts to bring our ideas and desires into manifestation.

Our way back into the Garden of Eden, our oneness with God, would be to understand and master the unbridled energy that the serpent represents within us. Sigmund Freud called this energy the *Id*, while in Buddhism it is referred to as *Kundalini*. Eve's unbridled desires, free will, and curiosity convinced her to eat from the Tree of Knowledge, and as a result, Adam and Eve experienced separation from God. Embodying the First Commandment focuses our ego toward seeking God and tames the serpent within us. Our commitment to meditate on the true nature of our being and to communicate with God directly, listening for the still, small voice inside, helps us on our journey toward self-mastery. This life force gives us our physical life, and we are responsible to choose how we use this energy to create in the world. It is our healthy ego that mediates between our life force and our relationship with God.

The Commandment Broken

Focusing only on the literal meaning of the First Commandment—not worshipping the gods or deities of different cultures—limits our understanding of how we may or may not be holding to this Key in our everyday lives. In a more contemporary view, by exploring this Commandment as a metaphor, we expand our cone of perception to include how we place many ideas, beliefs, people, material objects, or success before our relationship with God. It is not unusual in our culture to believe in one God who pervades the universe, so a literal interpretation of the First Commandment is easy to follow. Yet unless we recognize other areas in our lives that have limited our communication with God, we will never reach our true potential: to worship God, who resides within each of us.

When you focus on putting God first, you will understand that God is the life force in all sentient life. God is the Alpha and the Omega, the universal thread that interconnects all life as one. When we are disconnected from this truth, our own egos and choices guide us away from becoming enlightened beings. We are led astray and find ourselves lost in the wilderness. We are not resonating with God, who resides within us. The very nature of resonating with or attuning our egos toward God allows for all of our cells to be illuminated by Divine consciousness. Our mind, body, and spirit are finely tuned, our brains are actually wired for God, and our limbic system resonates this peaceful knowing.

Remember the research findings of Andrew Newberg MD and Mark Robert Waldman in *How God Changes Your Brain*: Our concept of God, as well as our prayer and meditation practices, can change our brain and enhance our spiritual experiences and sense of well-being. Regardless of our belief or disbelief, when we regularly pray, meditate, or visualize, our brains respond. I ask you to consider that when we meditate and pray on the Ten Commandments and focus on how our hearts, soul, eyes, and hands are affected, our brain and body will respond with several physiological changes. The Ten Commandments directly relate to our physiological, psychological, and spiritual health.

If we disregard the First Commandment by placing someone or something in place of this knowing, we begin to form negative love bonds (NLBs). Over time, the deep limbic system becomes programmed to bond unnaturally with a person, idea, or the material world, which suppresses our innate relationship with God. The ability to directly communicate with God is suppressed, buried deep within, waiting for another opportunity to express itself or to be restored. It's a fundamental, basic fact: When we break this Commandment to become negatively bonded to the thing we're putting before God, it causes a rift within us. Our limbic system doesn't know the difference between positive or negative love bonds, and it responds like a computer to the information given. When there is a breach, consider how this rift affects your cells, physiology, and memory. What is stored as memory? How does your brain adapt to positive or negative input? The answer is simple: You become divided within. The word *holy* means to be whole. When we connect to Spirit, we are healthy and whole, not divided inside. On the other hand, when we lose our connection and adapt to our surrounding environment and stressors, our awareness of the Divine within becomes buried inside of us. It is not truly lost—only covered, waiting for us.

For some families, this suppressed connection can be passed down generationally because of repeated trauma, abuse, loss, war, ignorance, and prolonged suffering. Understanding the spiritual truths that our ancestors believed in and lived by become lost until we search for the truth and wisdom inside. From the time of the story of Adam and Eve, we have been given this very simple teaching that opens the doorway to self-mastery and direct communion with God within us.

Stories about Choice from the Bible

There are many stories of our biblical ancestors finding their self-mastery and communion with God deeply tested, with various results. Abraham and Sarah longed for an heir, and God sent Abraham a dream that told him Sarah would bear a child, despite her age. The news was so incredible that when Abraham went home to tell Sarah, she didn't believe him. Instead, she took matters into her own hands and gave Hagar, her maidservant, to Abraham. Amazingly, after that, Sarah got pregnant. The birth of Hagar's son, Ishmael, and the resulting conflicts—still driven by Sarah—led to the genesis of two world religions from Abraham's seed, and the conflicts continue to this day. Sarah's mistake was that she didn't meditate and put her trust in God first; rather, she put her own fears first and tried to control the situation on her own.

Now compare Sarah's actions to what Abraham did when God asked him to sacrifice his son Isaac as a test of his love. He didn't want to do it—what parent would?—but he put his faith in God and put God first. He prayed and found it in himself to bring his beloved son to the altar. Abraham passed the test, and God stopped him from killing his son, instructing him instead to sacrifice a nearby ram. In metaphor, this story teaches us that only God is to be first in our life. We also see the rewards available to us when we put Him first. There is truth here, as well as the peace and security of knowing we can trust God.

When we take things into our own hands, as Sarah did, we bring about events that may, on the outside, look like curses. It may seem like God is punishing us. But these events are in fact consequences of our choices and the actions we've made. This is what happens when we don't take the time to be still and listen for God's direction. Consider a situation in your life when you didn't listen to God and tried to control it on your own. Chances are it caused a ripple effect of unforeseen consequences.

Tuning in to God

Learning to hear the unique way God speaks to you is important for spiritual growth and health. Our ancestors knew how to walk and communicate with God throughout their day. Listening, praying, and meditating were as common daily practices as brushing our teeth is today We have only to slow down, pay attention, and listen to develop proficiency on a par with theirs. God speaks to each of us in many different ways. Some of these might include the following:

Prayer. When we take the time to commune with God, we have the ability to ask for and receive His direction.

Meditation. In meditation, we clear our minds to provide a clear channel through which to hear God's word. In this book, I suggest that when we meditate on the Ten Commandments and practice the *I AM* Meditation to restore the Divine qualities within us, our direct communication with the Divine is awakened.

Our Work. If you're at work and having difficulty with a particular issue, you might take a break and later suddenly find the answer to your problem. You might think it was coincidence, but such epiphanies are the inspiration of Spirit talking to us.

Our Daily Living. The still, small voice inside speaks with us throughout the day. You experience a synchronistic event that makes life flow effortlessly. Maybe you get an idea or a feeling that your child is going to be sick before they actually do, or you have an inkling that tells you to take your umbrella, because it might rain. God doesn't have to be telling you something profound. If we're in tune, in rhythm, His voice is speaking to us all the time. When we're in the rhythm of life, things just happen.

The more we listen, the more we can identify places in our lives where we are out of integrity with the Divine within us. Many of my clients found that some of their symptoms were actually a signal that God was trying to communicate with them about their problems. Stress, depression, digestive problems, and headaches can be our body's way of communicating that we are out of sync with God. When we are in tune with God, our big problems become smaller. We tend to overdramatize our problems and make them bigger than God. Following are a few examples of how your very symptoms can be a signal for you to listen to that Voice. If you try listening, you'll find that God will resolve your problems and lessen your burdens while restoring you to spiritual wholeness.

Out of Alignment

Bill reported an uneasy feeling during a meeting at work and grew particularly anxious and nervous when his colleagues introduced new policies and guidelines for employees. The team had worked on these for a few weeks and wanted to implement them right away. Bill wanted to be supportive, yet he disagreed with several new policies. His attempts to communicate his thoughts and feelings were met with disapproval from some team members, so he decided to override his gut feeling and submit, in order not to make waves, to keep his job, and to be considered a team player. When Bill left the meeting, he felt uneasy, as if he had lost his integrity. Bill judged himself for not being an effective communicator. For the next few days, his anxiety and stress caused him sleepless nights, paranoia, and indigestion.

In our session, Bill realized his physical symptoms were directly connected to submitting at the meeting. He felt out of alignment with his own personal integrity and started to look for alternative ways to address the issue at work. Bill began to meditate and pray for more clarity on the issue and for resources on how to communicate his views. He used the *I AM* Meditation and the First Commandment to refocus his energy and mind toward God. By turning inward toward God and listening for alternative solutions, Bill's anxiety, physical symptoms, and stress reduced. He became aware that placing work, company polices, and others before listening to God caused him unnecessary duress and sleepless nights. The next day, Bill was able to write a memo to his colleagues addressing his concerns, explaining why he was uncomfortable with the new policies, and offering alternative solutions. His memo opened communication between team members to revisit the policies and Bill's concerns.

Out of Integrity

Tom, an executive from New Jersey, worked for a business in the Philadelphia area. Tom was asked by his superiors to give an employee a poor work review. Tom liked the employee and felt he did a tremendous job, and he wondered why upper management would ask him to pass bad news on to the employee. On many occasions, Tom refused, considering the review unfair. He received a lot of grief from upper management for not participating in what he deemed unethical behavior.

On his way to work, Tom traveled via the Walt Whitman Bridge. Each day, while approaching the bridge he began to have anxiety attacks and feel sick to his stomach. The symptoms became so debilitating that he decided to seek help. In his personal work and exploration, Tom recognized how his symptoms directly corresponded to his work situation. He had wanted to leave his position and was overriding his internal signals, convincing himself that things were bound to get better. He would actually convince himself that his superiors were okay people to work for, except in this situation.

When he recognized the situation was making him sick, anxious, and paranoid, Tom realized he had placed work and his boss over his relationship with God. Because of the situation and the way that many of the employees felt stuck, he had also placed his company position before God. When Tom prayed and meditated on what would be the best for himself and his family, he was told to apply for a position at another company. The following week he did so, and he was hired soon afterwards. Tom realized that his anxiety and other symptoms were one way God was speaking through him. He needed to listen more deeply whenever he felt under duress, and knew he would receive communication from God on how to handle stressful situations. His symptoms were actually the result of not listening and of ignoring his own integrity.

Out of Faith

Another client, Patricia, discovered her husband was having an affair. As any wife would, she felt devastated, angry, and depressed. Her life was turned upside down. She had trusted her husband and thought surely this would never happen to them. She felt helpless and depressed, and her depression seemed to grow. She kept asking in utter disbelief, "How could he have ruined our life together?" Her dreams were crushed, and she didn't know how to handle everything. She was a stay-at-home mom who had given up her career to support him and take care of their children.

In our sessions together, Patricia was able to express her rage and anger, to grieve the loss of her ideal marriage, and to face how she had placed her relationship with her husband before her relationship with God. She had put all her trust in him, and when he failed, she was devastated and lost. Her self-esteem was at an all-time low. As she meditated and prayed for strength, she realized that by turning toward God for support, she could respond to her husband's infidelity in a new way and work on their relationship in therapy before considering filing for a divorce. In the months to come, Patricia realized how despondent she had become in the marriage, focusing only on the children and neglecting her husband. While this still did not give him the right or privilege to break the vows of their marriage, she was able to understand that the situation was much more complex than him having the affair.

Patricia's husband had also become busy at work and neglectful of his responsibilities at home. On many occasions he had left Patricia, who felt deserted, to handle everything at home on her own while he traveled and played golf on weekends. He had placed his work and business associates before his relationship with God, his wife, and his family.

Both Patricia and her husband discovered they had lost their connection with God, which preceded their loss of connection with each other. Each one committed to asking God for restoration of their marriage. Patricia worked on forgiveness of her husband. She realized that as long as she put her trust in her husband first, rather than in God, she was unable to forgive him. Without God at the center of her life, she could trust enough to open her heart again and love her husband. Once she changed her relationship with God, she knew forgiveness for her husband was forthcoming.

This was an optimal outcome for this couple. Yet when two people cannot heal or work through difficult issues and they cause each other more pain and suffering, divorce may be the healthy solution. I mention this because some of you will have had an experience where you needed to bring a marriage to closure. It is important to use the information in this book as a guide to building healthy relationships. Whatever your history or situation, you can use the information presented here to open your heart, gain insight, grow as a person, and receive deep healing.

The Healing Work

God instructs us to meditate on each Commandment, to inscribe them on our hearts, souls, eyes, and hands, to place them on our houses, and teach them to our children. What does this actually mean? Have we tried to meditate on each Key in each of these respective places? The instruction is clear. Our Jewish ancestors meditated on each Key and literally placed them on their bodies. Later, Christ taught us that this work was already done. The meditations, prayers, and chants of our ancestors had actually written these Keys into the minds of all humanity. We are actually born into them; they are part of our very nature. God wanted us to know this truth. Meditating on the Keys today—not as laws first, but as a way to open our relationship with God and to restore our physical, psychological, familial, and spiritual health and well-being—is the message God was sending us.

Create some time in your day to contemplate this First Key on your heart: "*You shall have no other gods before me.*" If you want to, you can reframe the Commandment into a positive affirmation such as, "I trust in God who lives in my heart." What happens? Is your heart drowning in other things?

Do you know God is living in your heart? Can you feel the Divine love expressing through your heart? Take a moment to notice anything you may have placed before God or your relationship with Him. Do you have unresolved pain, guilt, anger, or mistrust in your heart? Meditate and restore the balance of your heart by placing God first. What is your experience? Do you notice how this affects your heart, your mind, and your body? What is your experience?

Now, move the First Commandment into your soul. Are you connected to God within your soul? Are you aware that God communicates to you through your soul's longing, desires, and dreams? Do you discount these impressions and dreams, or do you fulfill them by listening and following through? What is covering your soul or inhibiting your soul connection to God? Consider how meditating on the Commandment can help you heal or transform anything that covers or impedes your soul's dream, potential, or longing.

Once you feel the connection, move the Commandment up into your eyes. How do you see God, yourself, others, and the world? Can you see the majestic nature in all of creation? Can you surrender and allow God to look through your eyes? Maybe you only see what's wrong with the world, other people's problems, war, or crime. The evening news and newspapers are saturated with what's wrong with the world. How do these beliefs, thoughts, and images cover your eyes and blind you from seeing the Divine potential in yourself, others, and the world? You can often soften your vision when you enjoy nature or when you are in the company of small children. How you perceive the world needs to be centered in God's Divine light. This First Commandment is a way to cleanse our eyes, to remove the blinders, and to see the world as God does.

Once you have widened your perceptions, move the Commandment into your hands. You shall have no other God in your hands. Your hands are filled with one universal light, with all the gifts the Divine can offer. Your hands can create from the influx of Divine energy within you. When you block the flow of Divine energy in your hands, you feel less creative, less productive, and less effective in the world. Our hands are made for God's work, to fulfill our potential, and to bring all of our creativity forward. Just as God, the one universal life force, created all that is here, now and for eternity, we can diligently work with the Divine light within us to create beauty and bring peace and healing to the world. When our hands are filled with light, we can touch each other with grace. God's healing power is expressed through our hands, whether through art, writing contracts, healing, or plumbing. Regardless of what we are doing with our hands, they are filled with grace when we allow God to flow through us.

Another way you can begin healing with this Spiritual Key is to contemplate your family and create a Family Genogram (see Chapter 3 if you need help with this). Make notes of any particular relationship problems, such as divorce, alcoholism, death, abuse, or suicide. Place each family member on your genogram, and consider your genogram from a God-Realization perspective. Who in your genogram is disconnected from understanding this Spiritual Key? Did any of their problems or situations cause this disconnection? Take particular notice of who is connected to God through their spiritual practices, and note these connections. Take time to meditate and pray about each member in your genogram. Notice if you carry certain beliefs about these family members. Keep your prayers, thoughts, and explorations in a journal or your companion workbook.

In order to activate healing around any one of your ancestors, you can begin by focusing on the Divine qualities within you. Go to the last chapter of this book and use the *I AM* Meditation to restore the Divine qualities within. Then work with each Commandment in your heart, soul, eyes, and hands. You will open to deeper communication with the Divine within you and create a sense of peacefulness for healing your generational negative love bonds.

Once you become peaceful, pray on the First Commandment in your heart. How does it feel—on your heart, in your soul, in front of your eyes, in your hands? Are there any situations, people (such as your children or spouse), successes, or material possessions you place before God? Make a list for each area. For instance, you may focus more on the pain of loss stored in your heart than you do on God's love. Or perhaps you see others' shortcomings rather than their Divine selves, because you are looking through the eyes of judgment and not the eye of God's love and mercy. Use the *I AM* mantras to work on restoring the Divine within you. The mantras can help you to reestablish a sense of trust in the Divine, of humble self-love and self-acceptance, and of Divine self-respect.

If you get lost, you may want to reconsider the message that Christ wanted to impart when he reduced the Commandments to two, saying that within these two are the ten. The gift from our Jewish ancestors is that the Spiritual Keys are imprinted within us; every cell of our being holds the consciousness of each Key. You are born with the Keys of awakening and the pathway toward the Garden of Eden, universal oneness. Knowing the Keys and their purpose is the pathway to enlightenment and God-Realization. So, contemplate how the ten become two. Why did Christ do this? He tried to bring it to the simplest form—God and love. Although the gospels refer to all Ten Keys, Christ knew they would be hard to grasp without the basics: that God loves us unconditionally, and love comes from God. We are made of love, and we must love others as God has loved us. Forgive others, and love will shine forth. It's exciting to know that God resides within us and has given us the Keys to restoration, health, and wholeness. Contemplate this message and keep a journal about your insights. How do you experience God within you?

From a more practical application, do you overdramatize situations in your life, making them bigger than God? How? List the ways you daily become out of sync with God. What in your heart do you place before God? What's covering your soul? What blinds you? If you're in the mall and someone makes a mistake or isn't responding to you quickly enough, do you become overanxious and make it a bigger deal than it is? One of my clients, while driving home after taking her son to school, noticed a miles-long backup on the highway. She took a back road to avoid it but turned on her radio to find out what was going on. When the traffic report mistakenly reported the highway was clear, she was so upset that she turned off the radio. She observed her reaction and began to question it. Why was she so upset? She was on a back road and not involved in the traffic jam. As she thought more about it, she realized she was worrying in advance about an early-morning appointment she had for the next day. She wondered, "What if the same thing happens again and I am late because I receive poor information from the traffic report?" She realized she was worrying about something out of her control, something that had not even happened yet and might not happen at all. She decided to let go of this wrong assumption, to relax, to call on God to calm her spirit, and to bring herself back to a peaceful state.

The next time you are anxious and upset, take the time to slow down. Repeat the First Commandment or the *I Trust in the I AM that I AM* mantra. Allow the presence of God to be first over your anxiety. Slow down and ask God what is underneath the anxiety. Question what is truly going on within you. Your anxiety, emotions, and negative thoughts may be fueled by previous unresolved conflicts based in unresolved early childhood experiences. In questioning my client who experienced the traffic jam, we discovered that her reaction was actually embedded in an old childhood concern about getting into trouble if her father felt she hadn't done her chores properly. Feelings like this come back in times of stress, and we behave like that overwhelmed three- or four-year-old. The world seems too much in that moment, when it's really not. We regress to that previous state, to the original event that first triggered those feelings. But self-knowledge gives us the opportunity for self-mastery. Meditating on the First Commandment opens the doorway to our inner sanctuary and helps us to overcome our childish behavior. Do you ever become childish and blow things out of proportion? Are you overriding a deeper awareness? Record these insights in your journal or companion workbook.

A Helpful Visual Tool

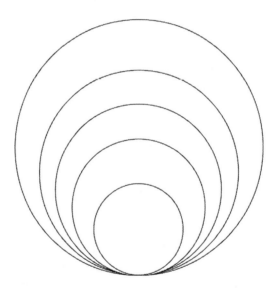

Now draw a set of concentric circles like the ones you see here. Write your priorities in order of importance within the circles, one per circle. Write your most important priority in the center.

What did you place in the center as a priority? Did you place worry, work, family, community service, or God? Be honest. What takes up most of your time? Where are *you* placed? Where is God placed?

Do the exercise again with a new set of circles. This time, make it the way you want your life to be. Meditate with these diagrams and ask the Spirit what you will need to change. Pray for help to make the changes. How can you change it? What resistance do you have to changing it?

When you've done this work, you may feel a sense of peace or connectedness because you're starting to become whole again. Or you may still feel challenged by the conflict between old habits and your longing to stay in God-Realization. Whatever you feel, that's okay. With daily moment-to-moment practice, you will move away from old habits and live more and more from a place of God-Realization. You'll actually reprogram your deep limbic system to create positive love bonds. Your relationship with God will be restored and become your foundation for life. You'll become the living waters of God's grace and mercy.

Remember to be patient. You may become frustrated when the old defense mechanisms, unresolved conflicts, and unhealthy beliefs want to hold you hostage to the past. Sometimes these patterns trigger us when we are with family members or friends. These old tapes can hypnotize us into a stupor. They become like a drug and produce their own chemical reactions in the brain. When you're under this influence, in that energetic mindset, you may become stuck again and bonded to the belief system of your family. One moment of practice most likely cannot make all these family patterns and negative love bonds disappear. You have to focus, use discernment and mindfulness to master these forces within you, and change the way you are bonded to others.

The Family Tree of Knowledge is both the mystery and the clue to your self-mastery and return to the Garden of Eden. That is the promise. God gives us many opportunities to work on this, and the more we do so, the freer we become inside. Our spiritual life is an ongoing daily practice, constantly being mindful of these concepts. The Keys make it easy for us, providing us with the roadmap to God-Realization. It may sound simple, and the process is simple if you want to challenge yourself to follow through with it.

Our biblical ancestors left us these Ten Keys, and Christ reduced them to two to simplify the process. Each Key is like a doorway into your wholeness and the fountain of grace that resides within. I invite you to embark on your own understanding and to deepen your relationship with God. Mastering your Family Tree of Knowledge with the wisdom teachings of the Ten Keys makes your journey to God-Realization attainable. You will become the One Body! Now that God is our first priority, let's continue our exploration and journey with the next Commandment.

Chapter 6

The Second Commandment: The Key to Fulfillment

You shall not make yourself any graven image, or any likeness of anything that is in heaven above, or that is in the earth beneath, or that is in the water under the earth. ~ Exodus 20:4 (The Everyday Life Bible: Amplified Version)

As we discussed in the last chapter, during the time of Moses there were several polytheistic cultures that worshiped many gods. The Egyptians, Greeks, and Romans all performed a variety of rituals out of respect for their gods. Their mode of worship was extremely complex: They paid homage to several gods who oversaw different aspects of spiritual life and culture—love, war, agriculture, the seas, the arts, and the afterlife, just to name a handful. Each god was supported by a mythological story and had specific powers. There were specific rites, rituals, and idols or statues to honor each of these gods.

The Jewish people considered worshiping idols and objects representing other gods or beliefs an abomination against the spiritual truth of one Divine Creator. Still, even though the only living God was supposed to be the God of Israel, the God of the chosen Jewish people, Scripture reveals that this God is also the God of Hagar and Ishmael, and of the Gentiles, and of all sentient beings on this Earth. Over the course of generations, many other cultures' divination practices, prayers, and rituals devoted to individual gods were discarded in favor of a Universal God or Divine Creator. Today, people of different faiths are even starting to consider the unifying principles amongst them. For instance, when I meet someone who is Jewish, instead of feeling the separation and differences between us, I focus on the fact that Judaism is the foundation of Christianity. In another situation, when one person can understand another's faith, together they can find a common language for the different names each of them has for God. They can seek the unifying principle.

Understanding our history gives us the foundation to understand and unify our spiritual lives. There are still pagan cultures in many places, including the United States. Some do divination, and others study and meditate on the ancient goddesses. Each one of us searches for truth and finds meaning in the stories of our pasts. All of these ancient stories offer some wisdom and teachings that outline our spiritual journeys, but as a whole, people of all faiths have become more aligned with one Universal Life Force and both the First and Second Commandments.

Why is this second Key so significant? Because it represents God's teaching that all our symbols, idols, and materialistic desires can block our ability to communicate with God directly. Although such items carry literal and figurative weight in the material world, they are not relevant to our spiritual journey. Focusing on the material world lures us away from our spiritual path and our opportunity for re-entry into the Garden of Eden or our renewed nakedness in God's luminous light, without any awareness of being separate or different.

To understand that all things manifest from one God is also Key to self-mastery and knowing the truth. God wanted His people to meditate and know how to clear their desires so they could be in Divine communion. This doesn't mean we should give away all of our belongings. It does mean we should not allow our attachment to belongings to inhibit our relationship with God. Most people misunderstand the New Testament story of the rich man who approached Christ and asked what he must do to have eternal life. Christ told him to keep the Commandments but then further challenged him, *"If you would be perfect, go and sell what you have and give to the poor, and you will have riches in heaven; and come be my disciple. "* (Matthew 19:21). When the man refused, Christ observed, *"It is easier for a camel to go through the eye of a needle than for a rich man to go into the Kingdom of Heaven"* (Matthew 19:24).

The Bible notes that the man *"went away sad, for he had great possessions"* (Matthew 19-22). It was his <u>attachment</u> to his possessions—not the possessions alone—that kept him separated from God. To contemplate this today, you have only to ask, are you attached to your wealth or material possessions beyond your connection to the Divine? Can you let go of the wealth or possessions as part of your identity? God gave you your wealth anyway. Of course you did the work, but do you understand the fundamental truth that everything we have comes from this one universal energy force called God? Or does your ego feel entitled to what you have over others? The awareness that everything comes from the Divine and never truly belongs to us is the key to becoming a good steward of the Earth.

The Key Learned Again and Again

As our Biblical ancestors have shown us, the Second Commandment often falls by the wayside in times of fear or stress. We must relearn it again and again. The Jewish people, as Exodus tells us, reverted to the ways they'd learned from the Egyptians when Moses went to Mount Sinai and left them to their own devices. They lost faith and demanded of Aaron, *"Make us gods to go before us; as for this Moses, the man who brought us up out of the land of Egypt, we do not know what has become of him"* (Exodus 32:1). Aaron finally relented and built the golden calf, which the people immediately began to worship. Moses returned and reacted in anger, but his people's behavior was understandable. He even convinced God not to smite them from the face of the Earth. Moses had been gone for a long time, and out of fear, the people reverted to what they had seen the Egyptians do: building and worshiping monuments and idols. They hoped this would save them. It's part of human nature to want to feel like you belong, to feel safe and secure. Reverting back to the old ways helped the Jewish people to do that.

How can we prevent ourselves from doing the same today? Our situations are not any easier, and we have even more images and idols to distract us. High-ranking officials and CEOs, those in positions of power, celebrities, actors, musicians, and famous athletes have all become idols in our modern society. These idols can either lead us toward becoming better versions of ourselves or—as is often the case—lead us astray into an unhealthy addiction. Addictions are unhealthy attachments, negative love bonds. The unhealthy attachment suppresses our real need for God within and for humble love for others and ourselves. We overly identify with our jobs and figuratively worship at the altars of personalities such as a Will Smith, Oprah Winfrey, LeBron James, the Yankees, boy bands, dance crews, and the multi-millionaires gloating about their homes on *Cribs*. At the time of this writing, a huge television audience is lamenting the end of the show *Lost* while planning their schedules around new episodes of *Dancing with the Stars*, *Survivor*, or *American Idol*. So-called "reality TV" has become their reality.

I'm not saying it's a bad thing to admire someone, but it's important to understand the difference between substantive admiration and empty admiration. It all comes down to our cone of perception. If we admire someone simply because they're a celebrity or have a lot of money, we might miss out on the deeper aspects of who that person is and what we can learn from them. So many people are fans of actor Will Smith, but are they fans of his looks, his talent, and his money, or of the whole person? What do they really know about him as a person? Recently, I watched him in an interview with Oprah, and I was impressed with how much more there is to him than what we see on the surface. He talked about his family and how each member is making sure that everyone aspires to reach their potential and bring the best of their gifts and talents into the world. Both he and his wife encourage their children to consider how their work can help make the world a better place. Which is more inspiring to you? Will Smith's box office numbers or his resolve for his family to make a difference?

Do you pay attention to idle idol stuff: who they are dating, what salaries they're getting, what houses they buy? The question comes up for many stars. Oprah Winfrey is also admired on a substantive level because she shows people how to reach out to their communities and open their hearts, and she does this herself in a big way. Brad Pitt works to help the victims of Hurricane Katrina in New Orleans, and he and his partner Angelina Jolie often travel to different countries and make a difference in people's lives. But the sad truth is that many people are more concerned with what they read in the gossip magazines about Oprah's weight or Brad and Angelina's relationship. What do you admire in these people? Can you see how God is using them to inspire and uplift the world?

Different people see different things in people, so ask yourself, "What do I see?" Does your limbic system go on overload for some celebrities and have you acting like a kid fawning over the Jonas Brothers? If so, can you pinpoint why you feel this way and what it might be saying about you? When Christ said, *"Don't hide your light under a bushel,"* He wanted you to remember that your light can be hidden under the bushel of family dynamics or under the bushel of your addictions, including celebrity idolatry.

That celebrity can become your *golden shadow*—when all those great qualities you see in someone else are already inside of you waiting to be born. Sometimes people admire other people's potential because they don't know how to align with what they want in their own lives, so they live vicariously through someone else. You might see and admire someone like an athlete who achieves something; he or she speaks to your golden shadow that longs to achieve. But instead of going out and putting your time into making your own dreams come true, you sit in front of the TV watching that athlete. You're not putting that energy into your own potential, into what God has given you, and you start to covet what they have instead. You live vicariously through that person. That's when admiration of another is unhealthy and empty. You may not consider the amount of time and effort each one of these celebrities has put into manifesting their dreams and reaching their potential.

When the admiration is healthy, the person you admire—like Oprah, for instance—may say something that inspires you to get out from under that bushel or old pattern you've been caught up in and try something different in your life. The connection takes you to another level, making you better and making the world a better place to live. The great lesson is to look at the things we put above us and see how they really make us feel. Does your admiration make you feel worse and dissatisfied with your life, or is it uplifting and inspirational? Are you happy, or have you disconnected from your Divine potential?

If we let go of our attachments to what is meaningless and go back to what is truly valuable—the God within us—we'll find peace and happiness. That is the ground we must stand upon. When we realize that all we achieve comes from the Divine, we feel fulfilled, and fulfilled people will give back to the world in a particular way. They help the needy and their neighbors, and they become even more fulfilled because it's not just about them. You don't have to be rich and famous to do this, as it also works for someone who has not yet achieved success or may even be experiencing a failure. You might not feel fulfilled in your life, but when you help someone else, all of a sudden you start to feel better about yourself. Giving back helps us feel fulfilled. We can feel down on ourselves, but when we connect to a cause, we get connected in a deeper way. I've seen people at my church struggling with issues such as depression or a divorce. They get involved in the ministry support groups for those issues, and eventually they begin to help others coping with the same struggles. Next thing you know, they start to feel better and start to come out of the darkness. They begin to realize they have gifts they didn't know they had, that they belong to the whole. They begin to understand this simple principle: Whatever we achieve is not what we'll take with us; it's the love within and whether we've made humanity better that endures.

Our Religious Symbols

Of course we can't discuss the Second Commandment without discussing the abundance of religious symbols and artifacts so obviously present in faith today. Do these symbols cause us to misunderstand this Spiritual Key? It's a question, once again, of attachment. Some people can be attached to the figure of Christ on the cross or a statue of Buddha and believe they are being true to their beliefs, but all too often they are attached to these images as symbols or idols without understanding how to embody the Christ or Buddha within themselves. For some people it is important to use these symbols as a focal point in prayer and meditation; we're visual people and it helps to have images to remind us of our faith in a deep way. Yet it's another thing to hold up a symbol like a flag and say, "See this? I'm better than you." That's where people create separation. A lot of religious wars have been spawned from these types of self-righteous thoughts and feelings of entitlement and separation.

Many people wear symbols and pendants to represent their faith, for Divine protection, and with a sense of religious identity. And many do understand the depth of the living Word inside of them and express it universally to others. You can see this type of behavior in many of the religious outreach programs. Others over-identify with their rituals and symbols rather than truly understanding the living Word within.

Christ could see how people misunderstood and struggled with this concept and wanted them to reestablish their relationship with God. He taught them that God isn't behind the curtain in the temple, only accessible by the priest. God is within us. Christ opens the curtain so we can have a relationship with God within. Christ is the one who gave His life to restore that knowledge to us. He told this sacred secret and reestablished the forgiveness for sins for all of humanity, not just for the temple priest to decide. While restoring grace to God's kingdom, He challenged the laws that were written by man and held in distortion. The second Spiritual Key is essential to understanding Christ's message that God is within us.

Images From The Grave

Today the term *graven images* can relate to generational negative love bonds that reside just beneath consciousness. Graven images can metaphorically include our ancestral images, beliefs, and misconceptions, many of which bind us to the past and separate us from wholeness. To restore health, well-being, and spiritual truth to our families, we need to identify, challenge, and change these ancestral images. Images passed on from the grave that inhibit the flow of universal consciousness need to be understood and transformed in order to restore peace and harmony to ourselves, our family, our friends, and the world.

Your Family Tree of Knowledge offers you the opportunity to awaken the Divine light within you. Referring to your God-Realization Genogram allows you to identify where you and your family need healing and restoration. If you learned from your family to worship icons, relics, or material wealth, it is important to see where this pattern originated so you can free yourself and your ancestors from bondage. We will delve into family patterns more in Chapter 9.

The Healing Work

Think of how our society has changed. In the 1960s, we had few toys. Our play was relationship-based, and as children, we connected and played with each other. Today, we give kids so many toys that they begin to think whatever they want will manifest. We've created a generation of kids who are attached to the media. They are limbically bonded to computers, iPods, cell phones, HD televisions, and videogames. They will even act out or throw temper tantrums because they'd prefer to be secluded in their rooms playing games instead of enjoying human interactions and relationships with the family. In many households, these objects have become replacement parents, idols for our children.

As adults, similar behavior shows up when we're upset. Many women and men participate in "shopping therapy," distracting themselves by buying clothes or unnecessary grown-up's toys. They spend a lot of money on objects around the house, but they're not dealing with the real issues with their partners. Some men feel insecure when their friends obtain something new; instead of being fine with what they have, they need the newer, bigger, faster, stronger one. Without thinking about it, some couples spend thousands of dollars updating their kitchen when they eat out most of the time. And unfortunately, there are people who will go into debt and damage their credit just to keep up with the Joneses. All of us can be seduced by the material world and lose connection to what is meaningful. When the housing and stock market crashed and the unemployment rates in the United States hit ten percent, many of us were faced with our own disregard of the Second Commandment. The bubble of financial illusion broke for many of us when the worldwide economy tumbled downward.

With so much attachment all around us, how can you work toward healing and restoring this Spiritual Key in your life? God directs us to write this Commandment on our heart, on our soul, on the fronts of our eyes, and on our hands. Bring your awareness to each of these areas and notice where you might be out of alignment within yourself. Be gentle and kind as you begin this exploration. Remember, your desires for material goods and wealth aren't bad; rather, it is your attachment to the desire that can block your entry into Divine communion. Try this simple exercise:

1. Choose any area of your life to focus on, perhaps your attachment to your house, your car, your job, or your idolization of a particular person.
2. Place this item, position, or person on your heart, soul, eyes, and hands to uncover your deeper needs and longings.
3. Does your attachment block your heart? If so, how?
4. Does your attachment suppress your soul's longing? If so, how?
5. How does your attachment affect how you see yourself, others, and the world?
6. How does your attachment affect your hands? Do you work harder to achieve your goal? Do you want things you are unwilling to work for?

7. Explore surrendering any of your attachments to the Divine within. What is it like for you to allow the Divine to be first in your heart, your soul, your eyes, and your hands?

8. Try this again each day until you experience being in rhythm with the light within you.

Remember, when you are in right relationship with the Universal Life Force, your desires can and will manifest in your life.

Again, God gives us clear directions on how we can either block or open communication with our Source. We are reminded to focus on the inner representation of God, to contemplate that which is invisible or unseen. Removing any obstacles allows us to become direct channels of love. For many of us, finding our true identity, self-respect, and self-esteem relies on our ability to communicate with God directly. Otherwise, we can become lost—as a person, family, group, and society.

Why would God be so specific as to make a law about graven images? He clearly wants us to understand the intricate nature of our mind-body-spirit connection. The very existence of this Commandment signifies what can disrupt the intricate web of our positive love bond or connection with God. Forming attachments to idols, negative beliefs or thoughts, or the material world can disrupt the deep limbic connection with God and others. Negative love bonds form when the limbic system is disrupted from its natural universal flow. Today we are inundated with addictions, obsessive-compulsive thoughts, emotions, and behaviors; the brain has become programmed to be fed by false Gods, idols, and material goods rather than by deep spiritual and human connection. The brain and deep limbic system actually become wired for the replacement substance rather than the natural endorphins created from our experiences of love, grace, compassion, truth, and mercy.

Was God actually giving us the keys to health by requesting that we inscribe the Ten Commandments on our hearts and minds? Does Scripture truly have a place in creating healthy thoughts, feelings, and behaviors? Was God telling Moses the deepest secrets to health and Holy Communion within? Was Christ's life, death, and resurrection the embodied message of God's grace and love for humanity? Did Jesus reveal the secrets of spiritual attainment by bringing wisdom and healing awareness of the Holiest of Holies from inside the sacred room of the temple to the people? When Christ gave His life for our sins, was this a sacrificial act that circumcised the heart of all people with forgiveness for sins? We have asked all of these questions in one way or another during our journey. Maybe you threw the baby out with the bathwater by thinking the Bible is irrelevant to today's world. I challenge you to take a second look… and then a third. There may be something hidden beneath your limited perceptions. The Spiritual Keys are right before your eyes.

When the Ten Commandments, the Spiritual Keys, are imprinted into our very being, any disconnection will cause a separation from the Divine within. To restore the heart, soul, eyes, and hands, we must come to understand the gift of forgiveness and meditate on each Key to open the windows of light from within. In order to be holy—to be whole and healthy in mind, body, and spirit—we need to restore balance by embodying the Keys. God gave us keys to health and well-being while helping us to master the force of unbridled energy that is within each of us. Each Key unlocks the greater mystery of light within you. It is your journey and awareness that unveils this greater knowledge. Acknowledging and removing one's attachment to worshiping idols, false Gods, or the material world opens a direct line of communication with God. Instead of blaming or laying guilt onto yourself, ask God for forgiveness and mercy, and restoration is promised to you. How does this Key open the light within you? Enjoy the journey and greater mystery hidden within your own consciousness!

Chapter 7

The Third Commandment:
The Key to Meaning

You shall not take the name of the LORD your God in vain; for the LORD will not hold him guiltless that takes his name in vain. ~ Exodus 20:7 (American King James Version)

Many people latch onto the Third Commandment as one of the simplest to obey. They focus on the profanity and take care in their speech to avoid using terms such as "Goddamn," "Jesus Christ" and, in lesser forms, "Gosh!" "Golly!" and "Gee!" But we also swear by the Lord's name in different ways that are also considered acceptable, such as swearing in court to tell the truth or swearing oaths to duty, such as when the president is sworn in. Which is right and which is wrong? As we delve deeper into this Spiritual Key, you'll see that it is more complex and harder to keep than you might imagine. It also represents our deepest connection with Spirit.

God surely wants His people to know how sacred the connection is of our lives with the Divine. Out of love, God instructs us not to use His name in vain so that we won't separate ourselves from His love and grace. The dictionary defines the word *vain* as "excessively proud, especially of your appearance" and also "devoid of substance or meaning." The sacredness of the Third Commandment literally means that our pride and lack of substance can lead to separation, pain, and unhappiness, out of which we manifest the consequences of that separation. When the consequences play out, we think we're being punished, but in reality it's merely an outward expression of internal separation from our true heritage. Remember, each Commandment is like a gift from God in the form of a warning, telling us, "When you do this, you separate yourself more and more from me." With the Third Commandment, God is saying, "Here's another way you separate yourself from me, by using my name in vain, thinking you're doing something for me when it's really for your own aggrandizement." This Key warns us to tame the serpent within and align our egos toward serving the Divine. God actually wants us to experience the light within us, and this is why He gave us these marvelous Keys. They open the doorway to communion with God and our spiritual awakening.

If you read the book of Ecclesiastes, you'll find its main teaching is the topic of vanity and how it has far-reaching effects on our human consciousness and health. *"All is vanity,"* it says (1:2, New American Standard Bible). In other words, all of our efforts, desires, and actions are meaningless without God, and without knowing and respecting that, we are nothing. We act out of vanity when we act as if we are the rulers of our universe and all that we have is ours by our own doing. All too often we forget to acknowledge the greater truth: that all belongs to God and nothing truly belongs to us.

This is why God asks us to give our first fruits, as in the story of Cain and Abel. When you give your first fruits, you're saying to God, "Everything I have belongs to you." You're being humble, showing that you do know and respect where everything comes from. Abel understood that concept. He knew that everything he produced belonged to God, and he showed it in a respectful way with his sacrifice. Cain, on the other hand, didn't understand the principle at all. He was jealous when his brother received praises and a blessing, and God told him to examine why he felt that way. If Cain had really looked within himself at his pride and his ego, he would have understood the concept, and he, too, would have been blessed. Instead, Cain ran off and, because he felt jealousy and the agony of not being special, he impulsively killed his brother.

It is a difficult concept to grasp, while we're working so hard to reach our goals, create our dreams, and make the world a better place, that all of our efforts are meaningless unless we grasp the deeper truth of oneness with our Creator. Entrenched as we are in the "me generation," we try to escape this meaninglessness by creating a society where more is better and everything is supersized to meet our insatiable need for more—all in vain, to fill our emptiness. We try to fill ourselves up with material desires without understanding that we have suppressed the Divine within, and that we are truly hungry for Divine grace and peace. Can you see why God would want us to tame this aspect of our consciousness?

Another Side of Vanity

Vanity is also defined as an egotistical disregard for others. You see it when people use the Lord's name in vain by following the Commandments with ulterior motives in mind or use the Lord's work for selfishness and personal gain. Often they are disobeying other Commandments in the process. Just think about the Crusades. Armies invaded other countries "in the name of God," all while committing the atrocities of war. A modern-day example might be powerful church leaders falling from grace. In one recent case, a man in Alabama had built and run a beautiful church with a large flock of devoted parishioners. But after his wife died, his life went into total distortion. He misused his place of power and position to sexually abuse girls from his congregation. He used the Lord's work in vain for his own personal gain. How many people are harmed, as these girls were, under the guises of "I'm doing this in the name of the Lord"? God isn't about harming others; people destroy people. God, on the other hand, is eternal. There is a huge, undeniable contradiction.

Although you may not have acted out in the same severe ways mentioned above, can you relate to this concept on a smaller scale?

Vanity And The Limbic System

When we become attached to ideas, material wealth, belongings, success, and our egotistical desires, our limbic system is affected. These desires can become a replacement for our real need for others and intimacy with the Divine. It is not that we shouldn't desire or accomplish goals or receive goods or wealth; rather, when we become more attached to these aspects than to our relationship with the Divine, our lives grow unfulfilled and meaningless. For some of us, the farther we venture away from the Divine within, the more ill we become—physically, mentally, emotionally, and spiritually. Our lives move to disarray, and we seek happiness from the outer world rather than our inner relationship with God.

In his *New York Times* bestseller, *Change Your Brain, Change Your Life: The Breakthrough Program for Conquering Anxiety, Depression, Obsessiveness, Anger, and Impulsiveness,* Dr. Daniel Amen correlates how environmental stressors such as neglect and abuse change the way our limbic systems are programmed. Our natural propensity toward healthy development is diverted, and the brain rewires itself to handle the stressors. To date, Dr. Amen has performed over 10,000 brain scans and has identified significant patterns that represent both physical and psychological problems, resulting in mental health issues such as schizophrenia, bipolar disorder, ADD, abuse, and addictions. His groundbreaking work offers us hope on how to identify and treat these conditions with practical daily exercises and or medications. He advocates that when someone's brain doesn't function properly, it is not that the soul doesn't want to be normal like everyone else, but the brain doesn't allow the process to happen. From my perspective, when our love becomes bonded with a negative event, creating negative love bonds, the Divine within is inhibited by the disruption in brain functioning. Rather than labeling some of these situations *dysfunctional*, we could find compassion and understanding for ourselves and others.

Our ego operates with multifunctional purposes. It can direct and tame our impulses toward healthy choices, or it can focus our energy toward unhealthy ones. When the ego directs our intention to search for God within, we become aligned to higher truth and wisdom. Our will becomes aligned with God's, and our desires are aligned with being in service to the Divine within and to all sentient life. On another note, the ego can align to our vanity and lead us on an endless search for happiness through desires in the material world.

Unfortunately, when we are saturated with the outer world, our unbridled desires inhibit the natural flow of universal energy that unifies us with humanity and all sentient life. Consider the effects of vanity on your physical, emotional, mental, interpersonal, and spiritual health. For example, do you overeat and still feel empty? Does your pride keep you from apologizing when you are wrong? Do you think you are better than others or that they are better than you? Are your relationships with others based solely on what you can do for them or what they can do for you?

These are all meaningless ways we occupy our energy and consciousness and inhibit our true Divine potential. Ecclesiastes 6:7 says *"All man's efforts are for his mouth, yet his appetite is never satisfied."*

Vanity also relates to pride, which is based on the human need to be special over others. When we brag and position ourselves above others, we will never be satisfied, and we are operating from the illusion of separation. False pride leads us away from true fulfillment, from knowing that everyone—regardless of their status or condition—is God's creation and is welcome in the Kingdom of Light. Moreover, using God's words and teachings to put ourselves on a pedestal above others creates unhealthy limbic bonding with those who submit their power to you. The person actually reorients from the light within them by giving power to the outer authority. The deep limbic system actually pairs love and submission together, creating a negative love bond. Instead of asking people to seek and be bonded with the God within you, you ask them to be bonded with your ego. You need them to follow you, raising yourself and ego over the wisdom of God within. Can you contemplate where the human egos of our spiritual leaders have led others astray? Have you ever given your power over to someone who you later realized led you on the wrong path? What did you learn from that experience? How did you feel about yourself and the other person or organization? From a positive perspective, have you bonded with another who has raised your consciousness and inspired you to fulfill your potential? Notice in yourself how you felt in each situation. What were your thoughts? How was your health and well-being? Which situation caused you stress?

> Ecclesiastes 8:14 (King James Version)
>
> *"There is vanity which is done upon the earth; that there be just men, unto it happeneth according to the work of the wicked: again there be wicked men, to who it happeneth according to the work of righteous: I said that this is also vanity."*

Consider this thought: *A righteous person can do something bad to a wicked person and be vain, and a wicked person can do something to a righteous person and be vain as well.* Each of them thinks they are better than the other, but in essence, they are both doing the same thing. Regardless of your position in life, you are prone to act out of vanity for different reasons, yet the consequence can be the same. Both people are disconnected from God within them and rationalize their position. Have you ever thought you were doing the right thing and later discovered it was for the wrong reasons? For instance, I have recognized that sometimes I share information about another person, and even though it is truthful, it is for the wrong reason. These types of instances only cause more pain in the end. I have learned the lesson of the proverb that *"only fools speak folly."* What are some of the ways you could work with this Key in your life? Have fun unraveling the greater mystery this Key has to offer!

David and Bathsheba: A Vain Offence

The story of David and his taking of Bathsheba is a bittersweet example of the complexities of the Third Commandment. On the surface, it looks like a simple tale of adultery and coveting because, after all, David wanted and seduced his commander's wife. But in this act, he also expressed huge amounts of vanity and pride. He was basically flexing his muscles, glorying in his position of having power over everyone. David managed to override his direct connection with God to get what he wanted. He put into play a work of Karma, conspiring and acting in a way that caused the commander, Uriah, to be killed in battle. When Nathan the prophet scolded David for his actions, it was David's pride and vanity he targeted by telling the parable of the rich man who took away the one little ewe lamb of his poor neighbor (II Samuel 12:1-6). As the story is told, David's children eventually suffered for his choices. This concept is important for us to understand today if we are to become God-Realized and heal our generational wounds.

In the Temple

When Christ confronted the temple priests, he challenged them for using the laws for their own purposes. Granted, the priests were sometimes acting out of the desire to enforce the rules for a safe society, but, as with the story of David, they eventually twisted their position to serve their own vanity: to preserve their power over the people and control the masses. That's why Christ was born: to introduce forgiveness of sins and restore wholeness (holiness) to His people. Christ tried to cut through their control with love, truth, and healthy anger—and yes, there is such a thing as healthy anger.

A Step off Course

Today, we repeatedly see this same example of a person of power or influence twisting the situation to suit their vanity. What's surprising is how much we're still surprised by it. At the time of this writing, Tiger Woods is the latest and most visible example. Wealthy, talented, and worshiped, he stated in recent television interviews that his arrogance got the best of him. He thought he could have anything and do anything. He thought, "I'm untouchable because, look, I've been blessed with talent and an opulent life style. Then, when his world started to crash around him, Tiger admitted that he had betrayed himself first, thinking he could have the beautiful wife and children and the sterling reputation, while hiding his numerous extramarital relationships. His attitude before being exposed was, "I deserve this!" Yet, sometimes when we're blessed in so many areas in our life, vanity and arrogance can slip us up, and we lose our alignment. Some of Tiger's childhood mentors are now admitting that their lifestyle and example may have set the stage for his indiscretions and arrogance around adultery. Because of these examples and his vanity, Tiger was unconscious of how to tame that impulse in him. Like many of us, he was reenacting a negative love bond with those he'd admired during his young and impressionable years. Yet regardless of his position in life, he was humbled by the Divine light from within. Like many of us today who struggle with our own negative choices, the serpent or life force runs rampant until it finally bites us where it hurts the most—right in our reputation.

We need to understand that below the surface, the light within us wants to bring peace and harmony. It pushes whatever is out of balance out into the open for reflection, clarity, and wisdom. For many of us, if we don't listen to the still small voice inside, trying to bring us into balance, the negative aspect will be exposed. This is how the Spirit works within us. Like Tiger, we are forced to take responsibility for our actions. He did that in a big way. If you are a celebrity like Tiger, the exposure is international. The pressure to take responsibility is enormous. And, although his behavior temporarily tainted his stellar reputation, it was much more of a deeply painful experience for him and his family. Yet he admitted that his vanity did get the best of him. When he was ready to see the press, he took full responsibility for his actions and sought professional help. His behavior afterwards demonstrated other aspects of his integrity, even if part of him was out of alignment. If our flaws are exposed, it doesn't mean that the light within us isn't being expressed in other areas. The light within us always calls those darker areas into alignment so we can be whole. It is when we take responsibility for our behavior that we can embrace true forgiveness for ourselves and restore our self-respect and honor.

If we listen to that uncomfortable feeling inside at the beginning, we will make the right choices, but if we try to override it with our pride, our vanity, and other negative behaviors, it will surface in these kinds of ways. People like to blame the outside world for their problems, but I say God is within you, and the reason problems get so big is that God wants you to see them. Mark 7:15 (New American Standard Bible) says, *"There is nothing outside the man which can defile him if it goes into him; but the things which proceed out of the man are what defile the man."* Are you paying attention to the signs so you make the right choices? Or have you covered up those signs because your ego or vanity wants something different?

One of my clients is in a relationship and trying hard to work on it. "We keep having these difficult conversations," she says. "We're up at all hours, constantly talking because he doesn't know how to put things to the side. He's always trying to make me feel bad or rotten." She acknowledges the good aspects of the relationship, but there are times when she feels so badly about it that her stomach hurts and she wants to run away. However, she does her best to ignore that feeling because she has a history of leaving relationships.

I explain that when your stomach hurts and there's something off, it's God telling you that something isn't clear yet. You don't override it with your mind by thinking, "Oh, I usually run away from relationships." There are two things going on for her: Yes, sometimes she does run away, but there really is something off that needs tending in the relationship. Spirit is telling her that. She must look at both sides: his issues and hers. And she must finally ask, "Is this the right relationship for us?" If it is, they have more work to do. If not, maybe she has to listen to her instincts and leave.

Some people can be vain and disconnected from God; some can be vain and connected to God. You can do something for an organization "in the name of God," when in actuality you want to do it for your own self-aggrandizement and further your prestige in the congregation. Again, it's complicated. In some churches or synagogues, certain people always sit up front because of their status, but regardless of their motivations, they are doing good things for the church and community. Their vanity may be at play in some of their decisions, but in the end, their money still goes to help thousands of people. Even if their ego and pride separate them on one level, their goodness, generosity, and love win favor. This concept can be very confusing. On the one hand, it can separate us from God, but on the other hand, it connects us. The scale is always balancing itself with our choices. If we want to have communication with God and we don't know what's standing in the way, we will block our own Divine communication. It is important to contemplate our motivations and thought processes. That good deed we perform may happen, but we might still feel disconnected and dissatisfied from within. God offers us this Spiritual Key and asks us to seek guidance, since vanity is one of the ways we lose our connection. God wants us to know and contemplate how our actions in service of our ego can inhibit our ability to feel fulfilled and know that we are the light. Dissatisfaction after success signals to us that we may have forgotten this fundamental truth.

Another problem arises when people only focus on the use of profanity while diminishing the psychological and spiritual teaching within this Key. Remember that God wants us to know the truth—to restore our connection with Divine oneness. The Key actually opens us to the light within by removing the barriers of our own vanity. It also offers us a myriad of opportunities to restore our Divine heritage. For example, if we apply the Key metaphorically, it is clear that teaching about God or spiritual practices for the wrong reasons (such as self-aggrandizement or personal gain) can be considered vanity and a misuse of God's teachings. To truly understand vanity, we need to contemplate how it applies to our actions, words, and deeds. We need to uncover our behaviors, thoughts, or beliefs that support a distorted position for selfish purposes. Moreover, we need to clearly identify how this blocks us from communing with God and allowing our inner light to be expressed. This distortion can clearly manifest in using God's word for our own personal gain rather than in service of the greater whole. This Key sounds simple, yet it requires us to be honest with ourselves and to heal any areas where we are steeped in separation.

The Healing Work

Sometimes we feel certain that our words, actions, or deeds are in the best interest of everyone. Only later do we discover that our underlying motives were self-centered. This is a good time to pray, lay our ignorance before God, and ask for guidance and healing. By taking full responsibility for our actions, we learn to surrender our vanity, pride, fear, personal will, arrogance, selfishness, greed, and ignorance before the inner temple of God's radiant grace. Humbly, we pray for forgiveness and guidance to make the crooked ways straight. Only the power of the Divine within can restore us to wholeness.

You can begin the journey toward healing this particular Key by asking, "How does my vanity limit my ability to enter the Kingdom of God and become God-Realized?" Can you imagine how vanity has affected your life or the lives of your ancestors? When you meditate and place this Key on your heart, can you uncover any situations where vanity has closed you off from others? How do you respond to others' vanity—with judgment or acceptance? Do you follow them blindly because you're afraid of your own power and all you can see is their power? Has vanity affected your heart? When you use the Lord's name in vain, how does it separate you from the light within your heart? Can you sense this experience in your heart? Now consider your family and ancestors. Has their vanity led the family astray in any way? If so, can you explore how? Does their vanity affect you in any way? How?

Now place the Key into your soul. Your soul resides in your high heart area, where God's true potential arises from you. It holds the records of all of your actions, words, and deeds. It is your personal journey; like Scripture, it is written into the mind of God (Universal Consciousness), your own personal Book of Life. How is your soul affected by your own vanity? Can you see how it suffocates your true potential or has led you astray? Has your soul experienced the effects of others' vanity? Maybe you followed someone and later found out they were not who they seemed. If this has happened to you, you followed their vanity, rather than their Divine self. When they fell from grace, you may have become disappointed or devastated, or possibly you woke up prior to their fall. Consider how following God's way without vanity opens your soul. Can you feel God's Divine light and your true potential? What are the aspects your soul wants to release so you can live your true potential?

Vanity also affects our eyes and how we look at the world. We often look at things, people, and the world for our own ego purposes rather than the betterment of everyone. Our behavior and words are cunning and work toward our vain purpose: to serve the ego. We may see the world serving us, worshiping us rather than God. This can come out in big ways if one becomes a corporate or religious leader or in small ways when we want our family members and friends to worship the ground we walk on. You may want to explore how vanity affects your vision and perceptions of reality. How can you let go of vanity and see through the eyes of God? All praise belongs to God first, for without God, we are nothing.

Once you finish clearing your eyes, bring the Key into your hands. How do you create things with your hands? Are they to impress others, to get approval, or to be seen for vain purposes? This is not the same as being proud of your accomplishments. We all need to feel the pleasure of our achievements. The danger comes when we believe we are better than others, based solely on our achievements. Yes, we may be a better parent, golfer, baker, or poet, yet our light is not better or more than the light of another. Our achievements should not be held out to make others feel less than whole. Each of us is gifted in different ways. We are born with certain talents, or we have worked hard to achieve a particular talent. Our gifts and talents are part of God's plan to build a better world for everyone, not just for ourselves. Sometimes, when we become successful we forget this very notion. Yet our success, money, or vanity doesn't earn us a seat closer to God. It is allowing God to work through us and giving our praise to Him that opens us to see others as equal on the path toward enlightenment.

Next, reflect on the Third Commandment by focusing on these three aspects: vanity, self-righteousness, and world change.

Aspect 1: Vanity

Contemplate and record times when you were adamant that your position was right, but later found that you were either wrong or worse—your actions actually caused harm to someone. How did you feel physically? Were there warning signs that you were off course? Next, consider the ways your pride and self-righteousness kept you from seeing the truth. How you could have approached the situation differently? Was there something or some aspect of yourself that you needed to let go of but didn't?

Meditate on the Commandment in your heart, soul, eyes, and hands. Notice what you do, how you think, and where you put your priorities in connection to the Third Commandment. Do you block your heart from loving, your soul from expressing its longing, your eyes from seeing the truth, or your hands from touching the world with grace? How does a breach in this Commandment affect your relationships with God within you, with yourself, and with others? Record your experiences in a journal.

In the last chapter of this book, you will find the *I AM* Meditation. You can practice it to bring about a change in your vanity. Before starting, consider a situation where your pride or self-righteousness has caused you problems. Ask God to help you understand the deeper meaning of the situation. Each time you say one of the *I AM* mantras, listen for an internal voice that may reveal more truth. It may say the opposite of the statement you are saying, such as "I don't trust" or "I don't love and accept this." These are clues to unraveling the underlying currents of your vanity. Stay with those statements; let them come up. See how they make you feel, how they operate in your mind and body, and then repeat the *I AM* Meditation again, so you can bring balance to whatever is unpleasant. Ask for God's grace and mercy to radiate out from you and guide you, blessing and healing your past, present, and future around this situation and your vanity.

Once you have completed the *I AM* Meditation, contemplate this Spiritual Key again, on your heart, soul, eyes, and hands. Reunite with truth and wisdom by respecting God's Commandments and blessings, and move your consciousness away from the negative love bonds you have inherited or created. Ask for forgiveness and mercy to open the doorway to freedom and release you from vanity's grip. Keep a journal of your experience doing the meditation or record it in your companion workbook.

Aspect 2: Self-Righteousness

You may find this difficult, but I challenge you to be clear and honest with yourself here. Choose one or two situations where you think you are better than a person or a group of people. List why you believe you are better. Don't worry, no one else has to see this! List what you see as the other person's faults or problems. Do you have some of the same faults hidden beneath your self-righteousness, or do you have others you hide?

Now consider: How do you separate yourself in your own self-righteousness? How do you contribute to the problem rather than help? How does your self-righteousness and pride keep you from understanding, forgiving, or praying for the other person(s)? What are the effects on your heart, soul, eyes, and hands?

Again, use the *I AM* Meditation to clear your mind and emotions. Ask God to permeate this situation, bring you more understanding, and help you to conquer your self-righteousness. Say the Key deeply into your heart, soul, heart, and hands to find and release any residual block that inhibits your communication with God. Record your insights in your journal, and refer back to your writing later to remind yourself how far you've come or have still to go in your spiritual journey.

Aspect 3: Considering World Change

Review one world situation or crisis, such as the devastating oil spill in the Gulf or the ongoing war in the Middle East. How does pride and vanity contribute to the problem? Did someone have good intentions and later discover their underlying intentions were based in pride or vanity? How?

Once you become clear about the world situation, can you describe a similar situation in your life? Again, be really honest with yourself. Use the *I AM* Meditation to clear your mind and emotions, and ask God to help you understand what you need to change in yourself to surrender into Divine flow and order. Is there something you can do now to heal or change that situation? Record your experiences in your journal or companion workbook.

When you have completed this work, I invite you to step out into the world with a new willingness to dissolve the separation that vanity may have placed between you and other people or between you and your connection with the Divine. Don't worry! If you can truly let go, you'll find that holding onto the separation was more physically, psychologically, and spiritually draining than you knew. Think of it this way: If you are 100 percent energy and consciousness, what percentage of your energy has been entangled in your vanity? Sometimes people spend a high percentage of their energy and time engaged in behaviors that separate them from the Divine within. Ruminating, criticism, and being judgmental are ways that energy is separated from Divine flow. When you realize how much time is held hostage to these unhealthy thoughts and behaviors, you can release the negative love bonds and free yourself to live from a place of Divine grace. It is your birthright to know and experience the light within you. Challenging yourself to transform the illusions of your separation from God will lead you to knowing the truth—that you are the light!

Chapter 8

The Fourth Commandment:
The Key to Peace

You shall keep the Sabbath holy. ~Exodus 20:8

Remember the Sabbath day, to keep it holy. Six days you shall labor and do all your work, but the seventh day is the Sabbath of the LORD your God. On it you shall do no work, neither you, nor your son, nor your daughter, nor your male or your female servant, nor your animals, nor a foreigner residing in your town. For in six days the LORD made the heavens and the Earth, the sea and all that is in them and rested the seventh day. Therefore the LORD blessed the Sabbath day and made it holy. ~Exodus 20:8-11

What came to mind for you when you read this text of the Fourth Commandment? Did it feel like an impossible ideal? Did you start thinking about all the things you have to get done on an average Sunday? Do the words seem outdated or irrelevant to your life? Let's put all that aside for a moment and focus here on two words: Sabbath and holy. *Sabbath* means rest and *holy* means whole. If you put these two definitions in the context of the Fourth Commandment, you'll see that this Key is really about resting so you can become whole. Being whole means having the Holy Spirit living in you and through you—but the Spirit is like a fire within. Any fire must be tended and fed. It also needs space and air to breathe.

The Fourth Commandment is all about being committed to finding the time and space to tend the spirit within you. God knows our busy schedules can lead to forgetting to spend time respecting and communing with Him. So He guides us to take one full day, the Sabbath, dedicated to remembering the importance of placing our relationship with God first. A day of rest allows our minds to pay respect with prayers of gratitude and thanksgiving. We can also take the time to listen for God's direction for our family, business, and community. Revitalizing our relationship with

God each week restores us to a level of universal consciousness that is imperative to the welfare of all sentient life and the Earth itself. Even in agricultural societies, our ancestors rested from raising crops and livestock or tending to home, community, business, and political affairs to appreciate and worship God. The question is, can we, in a society that commands our attention and fills our heads with endless chatter, do the same?

An alternative could be introducing prayer and meditation into every day, where we learn to pray without ceasing. In our fast-paced society, it takes strength and fortitude to pray throughout the day and to find the time to listen to God's instructions. The noise of our busy minds convinces us we don't have time. The pressures of modern-day living, household, family, and work obligations seem to take up most of our weekends. We may be well intentioned, wanting to rest and contemplate our spiritual life, review our previous week, and ask for guidance for the week ahead, but our busy lifestyles tend to leak into all of our down time. For this reason, we need to be mindful of how much we look for our spiritual life in other activities, such as seminars, retreats, books, and traveling to sacred sites, while neglecting to make time at home for this very private relationship with God. Some of us are afraid to sit still for more than an hour without anything to do. We tend to watch TV, read, listen to music, play or work on the computer, and talk to, text, or email our friends.

Yet, when we make God the priority in our day, our business finds a place of ease and peacefulness. We are open to new opportunities of growth potential. The clutter of our mind falls away, and clarity of vision takes its place. Our work is revitalized, first by respecting God and then by spending time offering our first fruits of the day, our love, and our commitment.

Planning on and spending a day with God each week fortifies our spiritual growth and aligns us with our true destiny. When we circumvent this grand opportunity to contemplate our lives, empty ourselves before God, and be replenished with blessings, our lives soon wander off track. We can't figure out what's missing. We keep filling the time with people, places, and things that never fulfill the deepest need to know and respect the Creator within. Allowing ourselves to spend one full day in prayer and meditation revives our relationship to God and sets our life in order for the following week.

Why would God want us to write this Commandment on our hearts, our souls, our eyes, and our hands? Is this a significant Key in restoring our relationship with the Creator? When we spend a day contemplating, praying to, and meditating on the Divine in this way, a direct relationship with the light within begins to express itself. It is like doing a clean sweep internally, giving you enough time to clear anything that blocks the light within from shining into your life, your family's life, your work, and your community. Take a moment to sense this Key in the center of your heart. When you spend time with your heart, you will understand what blocks your ability to love others as you love yourself. It's the same process with your soul. How can making the Sabbath holy honor your soul's longing and give yourself time to work through any soul growth issues? Now rest your eyes. When you relax your eyes and focus them on Spirit what do you experience? How do your hands feel when they are at rest? Can you understand the meaning behind God wanting your hands to rest from the business of the day? From the mind-body-spirit perspective, when our brain and body can become still, the presence of our Creator can be experienced and heard. We open ourselves to the experience of atonement and communion with the Divine within us.

The Limbic System: Forming Positive and Negative Love Bonds

God instructs us to dedicate one day a week in contemplation of our spiritual life. By keeping the Sabbath holy, we allow space in our life to contemplate God within our lives, to plan our life according to holy instruction, and to be thankful for what our life has brought us. The need for rest from the business of our lives offers us the opportunity to bring our focus back to God and our Divine heritage. Our brains and deep limbic systems need rest from stressful situations, challenges, work, and the material world. We actually reorient our brains to be bonded with God from within us rather than to the material world of attachments. Our brains need peace for our physical, psychological, and spiritual health and well-being. Taking a full day to contemplate spiritual matters offers us the opportunity to focus our consciousness toward deeper insights, wisdom, and truth, to solve our problems, and plan our futures. Spending a day in gratitude for all that God has provided us with opens our inner Divine heritage. The process of spending a day in worship also sets an example for our families, loved ones, and community to focus on the universality of the Divine within all sentient life and the world in which we live.

Commandment and Connection Broken

The symptoms that arise from not observing the Fourth Commandment can easily be mistaken for your average, everyday stress. You might feel a general restlessness and dissatisfaction. Your life may seem wildly out of balance. Maybe you are stressed to the point where you feel physically and mentally overwhelmed. You might even feel physically compromised to the point where you actually get sick. The next time you feel this way, instead of thinking about all that you have to do and what's not getting done and what's wrong with what you're doing, I invite you to stop and think about this: What is the quality of your connection with the Divine? I'm willing to bet that if you're feeling so out of balance, your connection is low or even nonexistent. Your life is probably out of order as well—meaning that the First and Second Commandments have been breached, and you have placed other things between yourself and your relationship with God.

But even if you're not in the right order, that doesn't mean you have to go beating yourself up about it or feel guilty that you're not going to church, synagogue, or any other traditional services. This isn't about making you feel guilty or bad; it is to introduce you to one of the Keys towards enlightenment and peace. Remember the story of how the religious leaders of Jesus' time challenged Him for healing people on the Sabbath? Christ told them that God created the Sabbath for man, not man for the Sabbath. He reminded them that the law was given out of love, for the purpose of renewal and connection. It wasn't created to control or punish them. So Christ challenged the religious leaders to reexamine their interpretations of making the Sabbath holy. I invite you to do the same. Decide what the Sabbath means for you and how you might create an experience of the

Sabbath for you. Think of it as another loving way in which you can take care of yourself. For some of you, it may mean taking a quiet walk, relaxing with your pets, taking a luxurious bath, helping a friend in need, or perhaps doing a daily meditation practice. When you reflect on your life, you may discover several places that are truly Sabbath moments. Be gentle, loving, and kind with yourself as you explore the Sabbath within your heart, soul, eyes, and hands.

Healing the Key

Our biblical ancestors had fewer distractions in their lives, so it was easier for them to respect and keep the Sabbath. The laws were rules for the community to follow, so everyone was expected to rest on the Sabbath. It meant they were encouraged to be in communion with God and to explore hearing the still small voice inside. It was part of Jewish tradition to sit, pray, and meditate on each of the Commandments as a way to open the gateway of light from within and to redirect one's life force. How can we do the same today?

What does it look like to keep the Sabbath in the modern-day world? Can you think of ways you already honor this Commandment in your life? If not, have you put off taking care of this part of your life? It can be as simple as being quiet with God at work or at home. With a little encouragement we can change our behavior to put God first and take *Sabbath moments* to rest and be in communion with God. Don't be afraid to listen to your own rhythm and explore your own ideas around creating Sabbath moments. I know for me, skiing at the top of the mountains awakens an awesome feeling of being at one with our Creator. I stop, weep, and take in the magnificent view of God's vast creations. Below are a few ways that others have found helpful.

Three Ways to Make the Connection

You might be wondering, "What am I supposed to be doing during this quiet time?" Of course, in our society we're constantly thinking in terms of doing. Many people find it difficult even to sit still for very long. But be comforted in knowing that in your Sabbath time or Sabbath moments, there's a lot you can be doing.

Prayer is what most people think of first for spending quiet time with God. When we are in prayer, we're talking to God directly, asking Him to intercede in a certain area of our lives. In the Bible, we are told to pray without ceasing, meaning to be in constant communion with God. But it is an active communication. Whether you're praying for other people or praying for God to be in your life, prayer is an action. Perhaps that's why it's the form of connection people are most comfortable with.

Meditation is about being still and calming the mind. Every religion has a different practice for meditation, but the point is the same: getting the mind to be still so we can listen to God and feel the presence of the Divine within. The saying goes, *"Ask and you will receive,"* (based on Matthew 7:7 and Luke 11: 9-10), but if you don't quiet the mind and listen, how will you hear it when it comes? A lot of people find meditation particularly difficult, even boring, because they can't sit in this manner. But as with prayer, you can do passive meditations where you are waiting to be filled or active meditations where you're expanding your consciousness to review a situation and get more insight. People also do creative visualization in meditation, focusing on seeing what you want for your life in your mind. You then send that picture out to the universe. You could be meditating on the next piece for your business, for instance, connecting to the universal energy field and asking for more information so that ideas for your business can come through. You will be inspired by being quiet enough to think about what you want to do, and that's not boring!

Devotionals may suit you better if you need even more to do. A devotional is a certain set of readings or prayer material that you have committed to recite on a regular basis, very much like a rosary or the *I AM* Mantras, for example. You memorize the material by repeating it over and over so it becomes part of your energetic field. You're devoted to a practice. There are many types of devotionals, depending on your religious background.

You can choose whatever method of connection is right for you, but first and foremost, you have to assert for yourself that Sabbath time is important to you, physically, emotionally, and spiritually. You have committed to the goal of connecting with Spirit, and you know you are worthy of doing so. If you understand that the Divine lives in and moves through you when you are at rest, you will be more committed to finding that resting time for yourself in whatever medium is right for you.

Getting Started

How do you take yourself down the path toward making such a commitment? Let's start by placing this Fourth Key in your eyes. Can you see how spending time to clear your vision will enhance how you see the world, as well as help you to purify your sight? Without spending time with God, how can the blind see? How can you see the higher truth and wisdom in a situation rather than looking at it from your limited cone of perception?

Now contemplate this Commandment in your hands. Does your work feel connected to the Divine? When you touch others, does it come from your Divine connection? You can take a Sabbath moment to reflect on how you use your hands in the world. What if everyone was so considerate of how they placed their hands? Just imagine it! All the abuse in the world would stop. Wars would cease. People around the world would come together to stop world hunger. Genocide would stop. Think of the possibilities of how we would touch each other after spending a day each week in the presence of our Beloved.

Think about creating a place of worship in your home. It could bear healthy fruit for your spiritual life, as well as being a wonderful example for your children and other family members of what it looks like to place the Divine first. Having this place in your home—even if you can't sit formally every day—can be a gentle reminder for you to create Sabbath moments throughout your week. And when you do that, you are creating a pathway to communicate with God within you. You are offering thanksgiving and personal respect for the light within you and for all that you have in your life. Creating Sabbath moments can bring you back into your center while creating a more peaceful state of consciousness. Moreover, asking and listening for guidance to create the following week allows you to move effortlessly into your week, knowing that God's grace, love, and support precede all that you do. You can rest your personal will into Divine will.

When you rest your personal will into Divine will, life becomes easier, because you are not pushing yourself to be responsible for making everything happen. You get to ponder, "Who's really running the show here?" Sometimes I think I'm running the show because I'm a great multi-tasker. I can get a lot of things done. But I forget that it's not me; the Divine is running the show. If I don't slow down and allow the Divine to precede me, I'll either get burned out or make poor choices that will require me to do something two or three times over to complete it, and it just takes a lot longer. There's a difference between having your goals met with effort and feeling like you're moving effortlessly. Sometimes when you're "efforting," your will is pushing you forward to get it done, and you're sort of running in front of God instead of letting God go before you. It's easy to fall into this place when you're in business or busy and people are depending on you. But if you're a really strong person, who will you depend on? You have to learn to let some of this go and allow God to pick up the slack.

So I encourage you to commit to the process and become dedicated to setting aside time to connect to the Divine. You can sit in meditation, reciting this Key in your heart, soul, eyes, and hands to find out where you are blocking the light and wisdom from emerging. Ask yourself, "Is it really possible for me to set aside one day a week to spend in contemplation, meditation, and spiritual practices?" Notice your desire and resistance to spending a whole day committed to knowing God within. It is interesting that we can spend more time on frivolous things, such as watching television and playing videogames, than communing with our Creator. Take notice of whether or not you are teaching your partner, your children, your friends, and your colleagues that it is nurturing to seek and know God. If not, what small steps can you make to move in that direction? Let your mind and body come into cohesiveness and find peace. Try taking *Sabbath moments* during the day to reflect on the keys and *I AM* Mantras. All you have to do is begin!

Chapter 9

The Fifth Commandment:
The Key to Belonging

Honor your father and your mother, that your days may be long upon the land which the Lord your God is giving you. ~Exodus 20:12 (New King James Version)

As we begin to contemplate the Fifth Commandment, we enter another level of our spiritual journey. If you look back on the previous four Keys, you'll see they all relate to your personal relationship with God and restoring this foundational wisdom truth: Your inner circle of life is to be in right relationship with the Divine within you. The next set of Commandments takes us out into the world, challenging us to contemplate our connection to others. We learn that the second circle of life is to understand and be in right relationship with our parents and family. We now move from the Tree of Knowledge in the center of the Garden to our Family Tree of Knowledge.

The concentric circles of the family history into which you were born are etched into the very fabric of your being. The light you are now emanates from the ancestral history of both parents. Your journey here on Earth is to unravel that mystery and become the light that is within you, to be born again of the light. Every family has a lineage of blessings and consequences that affect each generation. It is our responsibility to unravel the mystery of both our generational blessings and the crooked paths or consequences from our ancestors' falls from grace or profound forgetting.

Are you really ready to do this? It's highly possible that just reading the words of the Fifth Commandment above sparked some powerful emotions within you. You might be thinking, "NO! How can I honor them? Look at what they did to me," and that's okay. If that is how you feel, I absolutely give you permission (and encourage you) to skip this chapter for now and move on—until you are in a better frame of mind to learn from it. But before you do, I would like to give you something to work on here. The key word is "here." You may not be ready to contemplate this chapter yet, so we'll stay with what's here, what's now. What can you do right now to work on your self-esteem, to work with what this pain has caused you? Let's start with unforgiveness and how it affects your heart and soul. You can think about what patterns the unforgiveness is allowing you to play out again and again so that the pain you have suffered continues in your life today.

While you do that, and as we move forward in this chapter, I'd like to remind you of something else: The word *honor* means different things. The word *respect* has different meanings. You can honor someone for giving you life, but you don't have to honor their behavior and how they conducted their lives. You can stand in your power, firm in the knowledge that "No one is allowed to hurt or harm me."

For some of us, this journey can be very difficult, especially when we are stuck in a cycle of negative love bonds that hold us hostage to painful situations such as loss or abandonment; physical, emotional, or sexual abuse; war; and crime. All of these situations have a profound effect on how our ancestors and parents coped with the struggles of their generation and if they lost their way by forgetting the basic Ten Spiritual Keys. If we were the recipients of our parents' abuse, pain, or sorrow, our ability to adapt will reorient us away from the Divine within. Unconsciously, we bond with negative situations. Inadvertently, love and the negative situation have become paired together. Those of us who navigated this unsettling territory learned how to survive. Those of us who had a good enough family, with love and without abuse, may know someone who suffers or struggles with this Commandment.

For those of us who struggle, we often look at our parents from a cone of perception that is limited by past wrongs. I encourage you to expand your perception as you look at your parents and contemplate this Commandment. Once you work through some of this, you will start to open your cone of perception, and you may begin to understand that, in most cases, your parents incurred similar abuse and lost their sense of self as a result. They, too, have acted out of a negative pattern that has been in the family for generations. Expanding your cone of perception will help you release the pain and restore the Divine light within you.

Honoring Creation

The sacredness of creation awakens a profound sense of peace and belonging within our souls. Every story of how something came into being leads us back into a relationship with our Creator. The creation of Earth, the other planets and the heavens, and man and woman always leads us to the age-old questions, "Who am I? Where do I come from?" These questions inspire us to explore our relationships with our parents, our family, and our Creator. God wants us to know that honoring our parents is essential to opening the doorway of our hearts, souls, eyes, and hands so we can have a relationship with Him. Honoring our parents opens us to honoring creation and to knowing the truth about why we are here.

Moreover, honoring our parents goes beyond the daily pleasantries of respectful behavior. It requires us to explore beyond our limited perceptions of them and embark on the journey of awakening. The Family Tree of Knowledge and the search for God-Realization are held deep within the chronicles of our family history. Our ancestors wanted us know that our heritage is important to understanding the cycles of life, the blessings and consequences we were born into. The complexities of these past relationships do have an effect on us.

Today, we have the luxury of using counseling models, attending personal growth seminars, and exploring meditation and energy healing methods to heal and work with so-called "dysfunctional" family issues. In fact, it gives us a kind of comfort to classify the painful behaviors, beliefs, and emotional colorings of our family as dysfunctional, to place the blame on a definition. But people become over-identified with this term; it is one of the disservices the therapeutic community has offered, to describe what I now call negative love bonds. The term dysfunctional robs us of our positive qualities, gifts, and talents. It causes us to focus us on what went wrong and why we are the way we are rather than acknowledging that in some areas of development, our family simply fell from grace. When this happened, we learned to align and bond our love with trauma, pain, beliefs, and emotional colorings that were difficult for our brains and psyches to process. That's why I use the term negative love bonds. Again, I ask you to reserve the term dysfunctional for severe situations where people went out of control, caused harm, or deteriorated beyond functioning. Many of us function "well enough" or "very well" in several areas of our lives, yet over-focus on the negative events and disregard our gifts and talents. Most of us are not completely dysfunctional.

If you stay in this place, you will only continue to feel powerless and resentful, but you have an option. You can choose to be active and take charge of your healing process. The fall from grace or God-Realization is simple to track, restore, and understand if we begin to reclaim our heritage. Honoring your mother and father is how you will reclaim this journey and truly unlock this greater mystery. Consider that you can free yourself from generations of pain and suffering by reclaiming your birthright. Not only that, but you can also send healing through the generations and to your descendants when you embody these wisdom truths and master your Family Tree of Knowledge. I am not saying this part of the journey will be easy. It will require time, prayer, consideration and exploration, and a willingness to reframe what you once labeled as dysfunctional.

A Biblical Chain of Events

Now there was a famine in the land, and Abram went down to Egypt to live there for a while because the famine was severe. As he was about to enter Egypt, he said to his wife Sarai, "I know what a beautiful woman you are. When the Egyptians see you, they will say, 'This is his wife.' Then they will kill me but will let you live. Say you are my sister, so that I will be treated well for your sake and my life will be spared because of you." When Abram came to Egypt, the Egyptians saw that she was a very beautiful woman. And when Pharaoh's officials saw her, they praised her to Pharaoh, and she was taken into his palace. He treated Abram well for her sake, and Abram acquired sheep and cattle, male and female donkeys, menservants and maidservants, and camels. But the LORD inflicted serious diseases on Pharaoh and his household because of Abram's wife Sarai. So Pharaoh summoned Abram. "What have you done to me?" he said. "Why didn't you tell me she was your wife? Why did you say, 'She is my sister,' so that I took her to be my wife? Now then, here is your wife. Take her and go!" Then Pharaoh gave orders about Abram to his men, and they sent him on his way, with his wife and everything he had. ~Genesis 12:10-20

This story reveals Abram's undying love and dedication to God's guidance and direction, *except* when he was placed in a situation where he feared for his life. He sought God for counsel throughout the day and for permission before he proceeded in all that he did, *except* when he sought refuge in Egypt. Upon entering Egypt, Abram didn't consult God. Instead, he asked Sarai to pretend she was his sister in order to win entrance and favor into the Pharaoh's estate and save his life. In doing so, he subjected his wife to adulterous behavior. We don't find out until later, on another occasion when Abram asked Sarah to pretend again with King Abimelech, that she was actually Abram's half-sister (Genesis 20:12). Although Abram remained in God's favor, his family would still face the consequences of his actions and be responsible for repaying Egypt.

Later, Abram lamented being childless, and God explained to Abram in a dream that he would father a child, but there would be painful years ahead: *Then the LORD said to him, "Know for certain that your descendants will be strangers in a country not their own, and they will be enslaved and mistreated four hundred years"* (Genesis 15:13).

God was clear about what would transpire in the future for Abram's descendants. Abram's past actions would have a familial consequence. This was compounded when, without seeking counsel with the Lord and placing her love for Abram above God, Sarai offered her Egyptian maidservant Hagar to Abram as a second wife. By doing so, she set into action consensual adultery.

These conscious choices for adultery and betrayal created a myriad of probable futures, for which God was patiently and lovingly accepting. In that moment, both Abram and Sarai were blinded to understanding that their actions would be the cause of the enslavement of Jews in Egypt, as well as the creation of two new world religions. Like Cain, Abram and Sarai put their own personal needs before God and never searched for deeper meaning before acting impulsively.

Can you imagine the bewilderment of the generations who endured the enslavement and fulfilled the debt? How could they even begin to understand that what they were enduring began with actions taken hundreds of years before they were born? It's difficult to grasp, but we must all understand that we walk a path laid out by our DNA, though at the same time we have choices and opportunities to change the story at any given moment. Otherwise, there would not have been a Moses rising to leadership to help free his people or a Joseph who eventually restored Egypt to prosperity. This is the hope we all have within us, if we choose to seek it.

Forging the New Path

The sacredness of the family tree is visible within these biblical stories. Many of our ancestors went through problems similar to the ones we face today. Honoring our parents is the key to opening the doorway into our ancestral heritage, gaining awareness of our life lessons, and working on those lessons in order to reach blessings and healing. Our ability to express and radiate this knowledge in the family is imperative for our health and well-being. Likewise, the Family Tree of Knowledge offers us clues to the crooked paths that have led members of our family into profound forgetting, causing our distress today and leaving us separated from the Divine.

When we honor our parents, we respect their paths and are willing to look beyond their human failings to uncover their spiritual journeys. Only when we can do this will our lives be restored to peace and happiness. We need to recognize that in each family tree, there will be both Divine expression and human suffering. Every family has a history of the rise and fall from grace. This is the cycle of being a Divine spirit in a human body. In order to truly honor our parents, we need to understand the underlying causes of both positive and negative love bonds. In this search, we can become free and unlock the deeper mystery of the Divine qualities within us. We can restore love and understanding for our parents and ancestors while blessing our descendants and the generations to come. Our personal journey and work will have a direct effect on the whole family's deep limbic system and cellular awareness.

For example, in positive family environments, we respect our parents for giving us life and providing us with a secure and loving home. Even in cases where our biological or adoptive parents have failed, we can still honor our biological parents for giving us life and our adoptive parents for giving us a home, food, clothing, and security. In some severe cases where abuse or neglect was the experience, I ask clients to imagine a positive parental figure: a grandparent, caregiver, or educator they can respect and honor for the positive influence in their life. In these cases, clients can usually find someone who was like an angel in their life, someone who took an interest or cared for them when life seemed bleak and unsafe.

Honoring our parents (or parental figures) also provides the template for respecting others who are in positions of authority, such as teachers, bosses, law enforcement officers, and so on. Often you can track problematic authority issues back to a collapse of respect between parents, between parents and grandparents, and between parents and children. Remember that respect comes from honoring the God within us, which allows us to reflect love and grace toward one another. Any disrespect for God's Commandments will be transmitted to our children, who will learn to disrespect themselves and others.

A Disconnect from Authority

Everybody today seems to be in such a terrible rush, anxious for greater developments and greater riches and so on, so that children have very little time for their parents. Parents have very little time for each other, and in the home begins the disruption of peace of the world. ~ Mother Teresa

Here's an example of how this disconnection can play out: Insecurity in the parents' relationship to God is often revealed in a too permissive or too authoritarian parenting style. Either our children learn there are no boundaries, or they feel confined and rebel in anger. Parents are the physical representatives of God to their children, who develop images of God's authority through their relationships with parents and other authority figures. As parents, a conflicted relationship with God will be transmitted to our children in many ways. Our own guilt, fears, or unfinished business from childhood will be reflected in whether we are permissive, authoritarian, or authoritative as parents. Children learn to respect or disrespect authority by how their parents guide them.

When parenting styles are conflicted, children and teens may be confused, angry, rebellious, defiant, truant, or law-breaking. They may become depressed and or suicidal, and harbor addictive behaviors or personality conflicts that are directly related to the parenting style and limbic bonding. Children receive both conscious and unconscious communication about boundaries, respect, and authority through direct interaction and deep limbic bonding. Remember, we are innately wired to bond with love and at the same time with survival mechanisms. When conflicted, the brain registers and stores information in order to sustain itself, but this information may be in conflict with our ability to maturely bond with love later in life.

Our ability to bond in respectful ways is also dependent on our relationship with others. When peers and teachers treat our children disrespectfully, their sense of identity is infringed upon. Prolonged disrespect or dishonor can cause children to lose their self-identity or sense of centeredness and purpose in the universe, as well as their sense of belonging. Over the long-term, rejection by parents, peers, and teachers can cause maladaptive behaviors that trigger chemical reactions in the brain and set the stage for future emotional problems and negative thinking patterns. Instead of the child's self-perception coming from the radiant grace within, it becomes tied to rejection from outside, creating a devastating loss of their sense of self, which is usually masked by other coping mechanisms and unhealthy personality traits.

Honor And The Limbic System

The sacredness of our relationship with our parents is woven into the fabric of each cell of our bodies. Our parents enrich our lives with both positive and negative generational love bonds. The pattern of our family's physical, emotional, mental, interpersonal, and spiritual heritage lives within us. By understanding and healing our family history, we learn to honor our parents, and our days on the planet will be long. If we ignore the past, deny it, or pretend it never occurred, our lack of understanding and ability to heal our past shortens the time we have here on Planet Earth. This Commandment refers to our deep limbic bonding and longevity as a species. God gave us this beautiful Earth to reside upon and share with all sentient life.

Honoring our parents is more than just being respectful; it is about our ability to reach deep within our history to find true healing, regardless of the circumstances. Our inability to reach into our family history and learn about our parents' lives inhibits our ability to heal and find God within. Many generational wounds are passed on through the genetic and environmental makeup of our families. If we narrow our cone of perception, we limit our ability to find the depth of the Divine hidden within our past. We are left with behaviors, thoughts, and feelings that limit our ability to find and honor God within.

By working with the God-Realization Genogram, we learn to honor our mother and father from a spiritual perspective that reaches beyond our current memories or experiences. This process leads us to wholeness and understanding the true meaning of God's grace and omnipotent love. Without insight and clarity into our parents' lives, we will unconsciously form negative love bonds that will be recorded into our deep limbic systems. These patterns will change our cellular awareness and genetic makeup. Unfortunately, they are unconsciously passed on to our descendants. The God-Realization Genogram offers us the opportunity to unravel the greater mystery of the light within us.

Over time, releasing painful memories and praying for forgiveness and healing in relation to our biological parents, step-parents, adoptive parents, or caregivers can free us to find and embrace God within. If we do not let go of these painful experiences, we can be blocked from communicating with God in some of the same ways our parents or caregivers were blocked. I invite you to rise to the challenge of creating an opportunity for your children to experience a better path.

The Way to Healing

In order to venture onto the healing path, God wants us to write this Commandment on our heart. This Spiritual Key opens our heart to radiate the gifts of love, compassion, forgiveness, and mercy. When we meditate on this Key, any relationship issues, pain, and unresolved conflicts come up into our memory. Maybe you are plagued with resentment, anger, grief, or sadness, or possibly your heart is free and unencumbered. If so, you might want to contemplate someone whom you may have a conflict with and work through the stages of respect, honor, and understanding. It is important to stay with this process by opening your heart and expressing Divine love for God, yourself, and others. When you are working on a parental issue, stay focused on forgiveness and the Commandment. Allow any anger to come forth, but continue to ask God for guidance in how to forgive and understand. Ask God to open your perceptions to see your parents' lives. What caused the dampening of their soul? If you are working with someone else, you may ask some of the same questions. Continue to explore your heart until you are free from any negative love bonds that block you from loving others in their shortcomings or imperfections—something we all have in common.

Once you have worked with your heart, bring the Commandment into your soul. Is there anything covering your soul's potential? Do you have experiences from your childhood that smother your soul and hold you back from expressing yourself? If so, are these connected to one of your parents, or another person? Continue to focus your mind and expand your perception and to receive healing. Remember, you may not be totally ready to forgive another for what they did, yet you can still ask for forgiveness from God, because you may have held onto this situation for too long. It doesn't serve you. Consider how colluding and holding onto your own hurt and anger can be a pitfall, holding you hostage to past mistakes and taking up a lot of your energy. Ask yourself, "What is the main issue my soul is growing through by having this experience?" Did you gain a positive quality in response to a negative one? Have you taken on a negative trait, a negative love bond, and are living that out in some way today? Practice staying focused on this Spiritual Key to unlock the hidden potential in your soul. Allow your dreams and desires to come forth, and confront any of the negative images that circumvent you. Let God impress upon your soul your true potential and light. Ask God to free you!

Now that your soul is free, move the Commandment up into your eyes. Notice how you see the world, how your perceptions are shaped by all the experiences of your past. We look at others through a narrow lens formed by both the positive and negative experiences that we shared with our parents, caregivers, and loved ones. Notice if your eyes are honoring the other, or if they are judging. If you are judging, be mindful of how this makes you feel inside. How are your brain and eyes wired to look through this cone of perception? How does this limitation keep you from seeing the Divine in the other? Are you looking at the faults and limitations, or do you see the beauty of their light shining through their mistakes? Bring God's light and love forward and widen your vision to see more. Can you hold both the positive and negative aspects of your parents or another with love and acceptance? Can you see them as God sees them? Work on clearing your eyes until you can sense the light shining through and into the situation. How does it feel to look through the eyes of love rather than judgment, hurt, or pain?

Last but not least, bring this Commandment to your hands. How do you reach out and touch your parents or others? Positive touch stimulates the endorphins of love and bathes our brain with good feelings. How do you feel when you touch your parents or reach out to hug them? Are they receptive and responsive to your touch? If so, notice the peacefulness and joy in the contact. If they pull away or cringe, how do you respond internally and externally? What happens to your natural gift of love and grace through touch?

Now consider what happens when someone—one of your parents in particular—touches you with love. Do you respond naturally and allow the flow of love to feed you, or do you pull away? Notice how your brain is unconsciously wired to receive or reject the loving touch of another. Consider why you might enjoy touch or push it away.

Again, in another scenario, if you experienced hurtful touch or abuse, notice its effect on how you touch others today. Do you respond with suspicion and fear? Do you numb out and block any real sense of contact, whether positive or negative? Keep praying to see the truth and unravel the mystery of this great gift. Now, notice if you have ever hurt another through touch. How did they respond? What happened inside of you? Can you pray for clarity and understanding?

You may want to write down your experiences of touch as they relate to the questions above, in your journal or companion workbook. In addition, you may want to explore touch in your family as a whole. Who likes touch, and who does not like to be touched? These questions can lead you into further explorations of honoring your mother and father and your ancestral heritage, where touch and honor were passed down generationally. In addition, you can explore other ways in which your family expressed love, such as cooking, cleaning, working, and writing. What are the gifts your parents achieved through the work of their hands? What are your gifts?

The greatest gift in exploring this Key is that it leads us back to the Garden of Eden. When we honor our parents and our ancestors and release their crooked paths, we release the blessing of a thousand generations. We receive the prayers and blessings of all of those ancestors who have gone before us; their good deeds, actions, words, and prayers bless us. When we open ourselves and release any of the negative love bonds, we open ourselves to the greatest gifts from God, and we become one with our Creator. I encourage you to embark on this journey with hope, empowerment, and prayer. I have taken this path and have found God at the center of my life. I have found love and acceptance for my parents' and ancestors' journeys. And my father's true love, acting as both my mother and father, resides in my heart for eternity. I have been and continue to be truly blessed by his love and his journey. You, too, can know that God has led you to this path and invites you home into the light!

Chapter 10

The Sixth Commandment:
The Key to Respecting Life

You shall not murder. ~Exodus 20:13

The Sixth Spiritual Key is the simplest and most straightforward Commandment of the ten. But interestingly enough, breaches of this Commandment are also the most rationalized. God understood that we, the creatures He made, are uniquely endowed with a mind that allows us to walk on this Earth in awareness of who and what we are. We contain within us both the power to heal and the power to kill. It is one life force within us, and we have the power to use it in either way. But though we are lovingly equipped with this amazing God-given power, we are too close to the edge of behaving with animal impulses. With the Sixth Commandment, God wanted us to truly understand what we are and to respect the preciousness of our life force. He's instructing us to not take it for granted by giving into our animalistic urges or nature.

Just think of how close we are to that edge. The impulse can come up for the slightest things, like jealousy or feeling bad about oneself. How many times have we turned on the news to hear the story of a person robbing someone because they were in a stressful situation, such as a desperate need for money or having to support an addiction? The next thing they know, the robbery goes wrong and they're killing someone. The negative life force takes over, and the person loses their connection to God.

The first story of killing in the Bible, the story of Cain and Abel, was all about Cain's failure to master his impulses. Killing is an impulse, and when a person lashes out as Cain did, this awful impulse rises to the surface. Cain was told directly that he had to master himself and his emotions. Having the privilege of a body and being present in the world carries with it a responsibility to do so. God basically told Cain, "You have to go contemplate what I just told you," but Cain refused, and he had to suffer the consequences for killing his brother.

Rationalizing Killing

Unfortunately, we see this Key broken all the time in the world. We usually ask why or how did something like murder happen? Simply put, it is because we are different from animals in that we can think and express our thoughts. Unlike animals that kill for the sake of establishing their place in the food chain, humans kill in premeditated and thoughtful ways as well as acting impulsively. When we kill, we constantly try to justify it in our minds: that the victim was going to harm us or someone else or that they were keeping us from something we wanted or needed. In the case of war, killing happens on a much grander scale and can result in genocide or enslavement, as it has with the Native Americans, African Americans and Jews. We've used reason and rationale to make our case, but regardless of our motives, the impulse remains animalistic. Ecclesiastes tells us that a good person and an evil person can commit the same bad act, both acting out of vanity. We may justify our actions in support of our particular cause, proclaiming to help one group of people while exterminating or suppressing another group.

But whatever the reason, killing still has a profound effect. God told Cain that killing his brother would have consequences sevenfold. Even if we are unconscious of the acts of our ancestors, we are still affected by their behavior and actions. We may not be directly responsible for killing anyone, but our familial, ancestral, and national participation in war directly affects us, whether we are conscious of it or not.

For all intents and purposes, I have never committed murder, nor has anyone in my immediate family. Yet many of my relatives, grandparents, and uncles served in wars and faced life and death each day. The idea that murder or killing has not affected my ancestral tree would be an absolute denial of World War I, World War II, and the Vietnam War, during which Paul T. Evans I, Paul T. Evans II, Paul T. Evans III, Edward Lyons Clark, and Peter Sergeant Clark Sr. served in the armed forces. My grandmother Irene Evans dedicated her life to supporting veterans and firefighters. Many women also served in the wars as nurses, soldiers, and on the home front. My husband's family, Jewish immigrants from Russia, came after World War I to the United States, changing their name from Stravetsky to Strauss. Both men and women were exposed to the harsh reality of war and genocide in a time when killing was deemed a necessity to preserve their rights as humans. We are all affected by war and the consequences that follow. The hidden secrets, painful anguish, and post-traumatic stress have affected the very fiber of many families and countries.

This violence is still going on today. If you need an example, remember the horrific events of 9/11 and the aftermath of that dreadful day, innocent people caught in the crossfire of the wars in Baghdad and Afghanistan, and soldiers severely traumatized by battles and roadside bombs. Now there are people on both sides who will be affected for generations to come. Even if neither you or any of your family members has been directly affected by the terrorism and our response to it, you probably know someone who has been affected. Just as an act of kindness affects both the person who is witnessing it and the one who is receiving it, so it is with an act of killing. If we witness murders or wars and atrocities, or even if we just know it is going on in the world, we naturally begin to fear that the same could happen to us or our loved ones, and our vulnerable physiology begins to operate on that anxiety. The post-traumatic stress of these situations affects our families for generations.

The Limbic System: Forming Positive and Negative Love Bonds

Violence can have a devastating effect on our deep limbic system. God knows this and therefore warns us not to kill. Genesis 4:15 states that anyone who kills Cain will suffer vengeance seven times over. Does God teach us one of the Commandments here in the story of Cain and Abel? He informs us of the direct karmic consequences for anyone who kills. Many times the consequences can be felt and experienced by several generations. Currently, we know that post-traumatic stress reactions are directly related to experiencing and witnessing violence. The act of totally disregarding life and creation is a direct violation of Divine law and inhibits our deep spiritual connection with God. Our deep limbic systems are overwhelmed by the experience. When someone takes a life, it shows how far removed they are from the idea of a universal God that pervades all sentient life. They are truly disconnected from God.

Today, we can trace the history of war and violence within families and note its effects on the deep limbic system and brain. Several of our current psychiatric disorders may be traced generationally to either war or violence. Over time, the limbic system and our deep cellular memory adapts to survive. In Dr. Daniel Amen's book, *Change Your Brain, Change Your Life,* he cites a case client named Mark, a military veteran. For over thirteen months, Mark was under an undue amount of stress and anxiety that had reset his basil ganglia, the pleasure center of the brain, on high alert. In this way, the experience of war had changed Mark's physiology. Likewise, Charles L. Whitfield MD reports in his book, *The Truth About Mental Illness,* that early post-traumatic stress caused by childhood abuse is a main cause of most mental health issues today. Any type of trauma going back for generations can cause genetic alterations; our brains adapt to the situations and look for ways to survive. Our survival mechanism kicks in, and another host of symptoms can occur. In his book, *Biology of Belief,* Dr. Bruce Lipton suggests that the memories, thoughts, and emotions of a traumatic event can travel across the fluid membrane that surrounds our DNA. This consciousness has a direct impact on our cellular memory and can be passed on from our parents and perhaps even our ancestors. Moreover, Candace Pert reports in *Molecules of Emotion: The Science Behind Mind-Body Medicine* how our brain becomes programmed or addicted to certain emotions. The brain actually acts hungry to re-create certain situations to maintain a certain balance, feeding off those emotions. You can see how fragile our brains are when impressed over long periods of time with stress. Our natural Divine nature, our wiring for God, is mapped with these experiences. Our Divine qualities become hidden beneath a sea of this type of unhealthy programming.

Killing by Any Other Name

Why does God warn us about the impulse to kill? With compassion and love, God outlines a series of consequences for killing someone, but how does this simple Key become distorted for our ancestors and for us today? First, we need to understand that our Hebrew ancestors lived in a time where different cultures fought to take over the land, material goods, resources, and possessions of others. Throughout history, we can outline wars that were fought in the name of God and religious beliefs. This is a trend that continues today, fighting for "freedom and democracy" while acquiring the possessions of others. Yet many of us experience other kinds of murder that block our relationship with God.

We usually equate the word *kill* with physical murder. In contrast, many of us have experienced and witnessed personal or group *soul murder* caused by severe abuse, violence, criticism, and or neglect. Physical abuse leaves physical, mental, and emotional scars which can cause feelings of emptiness, guilt, and shame. Devoid of any sense of identity or wholeness, the victimized person may become depressed, and his or her life then feels empty and useless. Or they may live a life that is overactive and over-achieving yet devoid of pleasure. In both situations, the person feels false and disconnected, and nothing can fill the void. The loss of effective mirroring of the God-Realized self leaves a person empty and feeling hollow, as if a large hole exists in the soul or a large cloud of darkness covers their life.

When aimed at others, verbal abuse and destructive criticism have the same effect on a person's self-esteem, sense of belonging, and sense of identity as physical abuse. Both verbal and physical abuse create the same physiological responses and affronts to the brain and can cause acute or chronic post-traumatic stress symptoms, addictive disorders, depression, or other mental health disorders, as well as spiritual crisis. We may think that when such things happen in a social situation—such as when a group of girls gang up to pick on another girl—it is a casual everyday occurrence. Nevertheless, verbal abuse, destructive criticism, and physical abuse are the most severe affronts to a person's self-respect and respect for the God within. The abuse forces a person's center, their sense of self, to be moved away from God's light and loving grace to a guilt- and shame-based sense of identity rooted in a profound sense of gloom. This is what I call the *original lie*, which undergirds all addictive behavior, many mental health diagnoses, and identity theft issues.

Addiction is one way in which we kill ourselves. The thing we're addicted to—whether it is drugs, alcohol, sex, shopping and hoarding, eating or gambling—becomes our priority in life. It makes the addict kill off everything else that distracts him or her from or obstructs access to the addiction. The addict kills off their connection to God, family members, and the very self. In fact, the addiction shrouds or covers the soul.

The base note of our very being is about belonging. Cain, for instance, felt rejected, and the feeling was too overwhelming for his system to handle it. His fight-or-flight sense kicked in. If a child is feeling this on a certain level and the parent isn't aware of what's going on, the emotional overload can be pretty intense. The outer lie starts to become their inner experience and erode their self-confidence.

Verbal and emotional abuse happens in families all the time and often takes the form of scapegoating. For one reason or another, a family member is ostracized for something they did or said. Maybe they married someone considered inappropriate or they lost the family fortune or they offended someone's spouse. The wounding and secrets affect the family and, for whatever reason, family members move into that place of coldness and unforgiving righteousness. That person is kept out of the family circle—even considered dead in some extreme cases! This is what happened to my father and mother. If this isn't a kind of murder, what is? Such behavior covers the soul with the shroud of rejection and abandonment.

In the Bible, this is what happened to Joseph. Out of jealousy and hatred for Joseph, his eight half-brothers plotted to kill him, but Joseph's oldest half-brother knew this was against God's law and managed to stop his brothers. Instead, they decided to sell Joseph to gypsies and report to their father that he was missing and dead. This type of rejection can either lead to deep pain and a soul death or, as in Joseph's case, to a person fulfilling his destiny. Although he suffered, Joseph's trust and faith in God and his gift of reading dreams restored Egypt from Abram's karma. He later forgave and healed the relationship with his family. Why? How? Because Joseph never forgot his connection, he listened to and was in tune with God.

The Healing Work

Our ancestors knew the importance of repentance, atonement, prayer, and blessings to having a healthy family and social life. These rituals were openly shared with each other, and the community was an important part of holding one's spiritual life and commitment. I encourage you to discover the best parts of these teachings to help you examine where healing needs to happen within you and your family.

You can begin by taking responsibility for your actions, words, and deeds. You'll especially want to look at this if you've directed negative behavior toward another person—a family member, for instance. This is the first step toward healing scapegoat behaviors. Placing our sins onto another person or member in the family is like cursing them and sending them out into the wilderness. Continuously blaming others for your faults or problems will set into action negative consequences for everyone. The negative consequences will be seen for generations until the original problem is healed or a new family member is born to resolve it. This is why our Jewish ancestors honored purification processes for the emotional, mental, and moral well-being of the community. They knew the importance of cleansing one's soul and making amends.

I invite you to meditate on this Spiritual Key, to recognize how it has affected your heart, soul, eyes, and hands. Contemplate how it has affected your children and those around you. How has murder (in all of its ways) affected your heart, your soul, your eyes (the way you see the world and process information), and your hands? Has it had a direct effect on your children or grandchildren? Who in your family seems to be carrying this burden?

Contemplate your family tree (see Chapter 3 on the God-Realization Genogram) and answer the following questions in your journal:

1. Make a list of any abusive, critical, or harmful actions, words, or deeds that caused you or others in your family emotional, mental, or physical pain.
2. How many generations back in history can you trace this pattern?

3. Do you carry any of the traits, beliefs, behaviors, or emotional colorings of the abusive person(s)? If so, what aspects do you carry today?
4. How have these actions affected you as a person?
5. Do you have any painful memories that inhibit your soul from growing? If so, in what way do you perceive this painful event is inhibiting you?
6. What aspect of your soul (if any) was lost?
7. Once you identify any breaches, set up a time to pray and meditate on each one. Use the Spiritual Key to open the doorway to your heart, soul, eyes, and hands.

Next, go to Chapter 15 in this book or refer to my book, *Restoring Our Divine Nature: The I AM Meditation Workbook.* Use the *I AM* Meditation to balance your mind and emotions before contemplating the above questions on the effects of killing within your family. Ask God to give you insight and teach you forgiveness and understanding. Who needs forgiveness? Ask that anything hidden will be revealed to you so the "crooked ways can be made straight." Contemplate the following questions:

1. When do you act impulsively on emotions and thoughts that flood you with despair, jealousy, and rage?
2. How do you kill off your intuitive connection with God's instructions?
3. Do you project your rage onto someone else because your emotions are intolerable? If so, what happens when you do?

Above all, carry with you the lesson to be respectful of all life. We must teach our children to do the same, to be in awe of all life. To a certain extent, most children already are. Children delight in the sound of a bird singing, the rain making mud on the ground, and the waves coming in from the ocean. All we have to do is help them not to lose touch with that inner knowing.

Life includes this planet we live on. The ecosystem is very much a part of our being. Without our planet, we can't have clean water to drink or air to breathe. Without the honeybees, flowers and plants don't get pollinated, and we can't grow food. We are part of the Earth, and we must understand that when we put plastic bags in the ground, they don't disintegrate for a thousand years. We don't respect our world by polluting the water or by throwing out trash and stuffing landfills. The Native Americans knew this truth and even today honor the sacredness of our Mother Earth and all of its inhabitants.

At the time of this writing, the United States is dealing with the oil spill in the Gulf. Why did it happen? Someone didn't respect the ocean and the life within it. Someone didn't want to spend money for one safety mechanism. Buddhists teach that everything belongs to the one consciousness. If we lose the trees, we lose the lungs of our planet and our life. If we pump toxins into the atmosphere, we put a hole into the ozone. When we dump oil in the ocean, we kill our ecosystem and affect thousands of human lives and kill off life in our oceans. If we kill, directly or indirectly, we lose a part of ourselves. We need to expand our awareness to include the wisdom of how life on earth is interconnected. The universe and all of its inhabitants are interdependent. If we don't understand this concept, how can we ever truly hope for the best within ourselves, for our family and, in turn, for the world? In our ignorance, greed and selfishness we have the power to kill off our very existence. We may become extinct if we disregard the wisdom spoken within this fundamental Key. Honoring all of life and understanding that we are all part of the Universal Consciousness can have an impact on taming the killer within us all. What a wonderful Key to place on your heart, soul, eyes, and hands, and teach to your descendants! What does it mean to truly embody this Key? Give it a try and unravel a deeper mystery within you!

Chapter 11

The Seventh Commandment:
The Key to Unity

You shall not commit adultery. ~Exodus 20:14

*For this reason a man will leave his father and mother and be united
to his wife, and they will become one flesh. ~ Genesis 2:24*

There's been so much talk in politics and the media about what is and isn't marriage that it seems we've lost track of the essential aspect of marriage, the one that truly gives marriage its meaning: unity. Remember, God is constantly seeking to connect us to Him, to keep us in communication with our Divinity at all times. Marriage is another way God enables us to make that connection. The unity of man and woman is a joining of the light within each of them to become one in the light of our Creator. In today's world, we understand that the joining of light as well as the human struggles with this Key can be the same in same-sex marriages. Although building a family can be complex in same-sex marriages, the same principles of adultery and unity apply. Through marriage, we are to experience the unity we once felt when we were one with God. Genesis 24-25 tells us that in marriage we are to become one without shame.

Today, however, the sacredness of the marriage process has been lost, buried beneath the complexities of our lifestyles and the misrepresentation of sacred knowledge. Recent studies show that 45 to 55 percent of married women and 50 to 60 percent of married men engage in extramarital sex at some time or another during their relationship (Atwood & Schwartz). Adultery is looked at with laughter in films such as *It's Complicated*, starring Meryl Streep and Alec Baldwin, and *Along Came Polly* with Jennifer Aniston and Ben Stiller. Or it may even be seen as true romance, such as in *The Bridges of Madison County* with Meryl Streep and Clint Eastwood. When we become casual about and desensitized to extramarital sex, we become casual about and blinded to the damage it can do. Both Moses and Christ taught us the importance of keeping the family whole and holy, and how doing so would depend on understanding how adultery tries to destroy the marital relationship. Breaking this Spiritual Key by following our impulses causes us to betray the light within us, the light within our partner, and the light within our children and descendants. This disruption creates a kind of fog over the hearts, souls, eyes, and hands and of all involved—directly or indirectly. It violates our relationship with the Divine within others and ourselves. The consequences are passed down generationally and can have far-reaching consequences.

Our lessons from the previous Commandments have prepared us for this understanding. In the first four Spiritual Keys, God speaks to us directly about our relationship to the light within us: We are to remember that we are one with God. Our knowledge and respect of this light is the foundation for our life and our relationships with others. In the Fifth Spiritual Key, God prompts us to understand our family heritage and the Family Tree of Knowledge. As we honor our parents, we begin to make the journey back into the Garden of Eden and embark upon our physical, psychological, interpersonal, and spiritual growth into adulthood. We prepare to bring our spiritual and family knowledge to join with another. Now we are ready for the sacred journey of marriage and creating our own family. We join with another's light, love, and respect in order to create a family and build upon the Family Tree of Knowledge. Then, in the Seventh Spiritual Key, God wants us to know how adultery affects the family tree and our spiritual heritage for generations to come.

First, think about the light. When you join in that luminosity, join with another's light, love, and respect, there's a connection of oneness. Imagine one body of light, glowing and full of loving power. Both of you become one body without shame. Then, because of an extramarital affair, this extra person comes into your marriage and disrupts the unity you created. Some of your light and energy moves toward the extra person. When this occurs, the amount of light and love available to your spouse and family isn't there, and it's split. You become preoccupied with the other person, holding secrets, and sneaking around. You may not realize how split inside you have become. You lose a sense of connection to the God within you and your own integrity. You may even feel bad yet convince yourself that it is okay if your partner and family are none the wiser. In reality, the trust between you, your spouse, and children is now broken and hidden beneath a series of lies and betrayal. When it is exposed, everyone involved feels the repercussions. The consequences are forever folding outward.

For example, Tiger Woods's extramarital affairs put him in a place where he now has to deal with the far-reaching consequences for his children as well as himself. In fact, he may not fully know how his children will be affected until later. The base note for their home has been disrupted, and how the family will bond has forever been changed. Tiger shows great remorse and self-responsibility for his deceptive actions, which plays an important part in healing and forgiveness. Understanding God's message about adultery goes beyond the heartache and pain that is causes; it actually breaks the harmonious unity that was meant to be shared within a family. Shame now clouds over the light and can only be restored by taking responsibility, understanding the underlying cause, reclaiming the light, and asking for God and others for forgiveness.

This process of marriage or communion provides the basis of our co-creation with God to conceive children and create a family. We need to understand that the very nature of the joining of light is fundamental to our child's physical, mental, emotional, and spiritual health. It is interwoven into the very fabric of their being. Each cell grows with the innate knowledge of this oneness. You are actually born into your Family Tree of Knowledge. So consider why God wants us to understand how the act of adultery creates a ripple effect in the unified field of oneness in a marriage without shame. The crooked paths of our choices have an effect on our partners, our children, our extended family members, our friends, our colleagues, and our community. With this Key, God wants us to understand how extramarital affairs lead us away from our own integrity and light within. It is one way our Divine light can hide under a bushel of betrayal that creates generational consequences.

Of course, the consequences today are not what they once were. Most of us learned the harsh reality of adultery from our biblical ancestors without ever contemplating the fundamental truths hidden within the Key. There are many forms of adultery mentioned in the Bible, but the main reference is about seeking sexual gratification outside of marriage. In biblical times, marriage was considered sacred, a lifelong commitment. Betrayal of a spouse usually meant death for both people caught in the act. For the Jewish people,

> **Leviticus 20:10**
> *If a man commits adultery with an-other man's wife—with the wife of his neighbor—both the adulterer and the adulteress must be put to death."*

the harshness of death as a penalty showed the impact of immoral behavior on one's spiritual life, family commitment, and the community.

But with the harshness of the law, we lost connection to the deeper meaning held within the Key. Like our ancestors, some of us obey the law because we fear punishment, not because we understand the meaning of becoming one without shame and how this relates to our health and well-being as a family. Christ understood the deeper meaning of being one body of light without shame. He understood the human distortions that were ensnarled with keeping the Commandments. And He changed history by introducing forgiveness rather than death for breaking the Commandments, and calls each of us home and into the light.

Adultery, however, was at the center of many prominent Bible stories. As mentioned in an earlier chapter, Abram persuaded his wife to become adulterous with the Pharaoh. She did the same when she convinced Abram to try to conceive a child with her servant. David sought to divide Bathsheba from her husband, and Solomon, like many other leaders and kings, had multiple wives and concubines. On the other hand, there's the story of Mary and Joseph. Mary conceived a child that was not Joseph's. Legally and otherwise, he would have been entitled to turn away from her—and many, no doubt, encouraged him to do so. But Joseph didn't turn away from Mary. Listening to

Divine guidance, Joseph married her and restored the respect and honor of the family circle. His actions mirrored the forgiveness Christ would later mirror for us all.

Adultery as Soul Loss

The sacredness of our relationship with God is secured when we understand the true meaning of each of the Commandments. When we adulterate our relationship to the Divine light within us, our heart and soul becomes enshrouded with the deception. Perhaps, as in my situation, adultery was a generational negative love bond that supported years of excommunication from both the maternal and paternal primary family. Rumors are told that long ago in my family history, my mother's paternal grandmother also committed adultery. Both my father and mother were disowned or outcast from their family. The hidden secrets, untold stories and isolation were part the *family mind field* waiting for healing. They shroud over the souls of the next several generations until the light within someone is strong enough to unravel the greater mystery of light within the family. Some family members never recover from this type of rejection. The soul longs to be loved and the shroud of rejection hovers around the person and family until restoration of the Divine happens.

If we seek to understand the essence of this Commandment, we can learn how adultery distorts our integrity and eliminates our partners' choice as to whether they want to stay in the marriage or file for a divorce. For some people divorce is the right choice, and for others, learning to become one without shame might be the next step to finding true happiness in the marriage.

Adultery and Family Consequences

As stated previously, in my own Family Tree of Knowledge, adultery was an underlying theme that had far-reaching effects on my siblings and me. It seemed to plague our family and isolate us from any relatives other than my father. Although I was born of light, my innocence and grace were covered by the consequences of my father's exile from his adoptive family and my mother's affair. Soon after my birth, my mom was misdiagnosed with schizophrenia and placed in a mental institution. Later, we discovered she had bipolar disorder and suffered from post-partum depression. Anyway, when I was nine months old, my father divorced her, assumed custody of all three children including me, and disappeared with us to another state. Today, our pictures might be seen on the side of a milk carton as missing children, but this was in 1957-58. Throughout all this, my father kept the secret that I was not his biological child. He was determined to restore respect and honor to his family.

Years later, I outlined my father's life on a Family Genogram for a family therapy class I was taking at Hahnemann University in Philadelphia. Although I didn't know my maternal or paternal grandparents, it became apparent to me that my father was repeating a pattern with women that directly related to his adoptive mother. A wealthy Philadelphia family had adopted him in 1925. As previously told, his adoptive father passed away when he was thirteen years old, depriving him of the masculine guidance boys crave and need during the important and impressionable teenage years. He went to Penn Charter, a private school in Philadelphia, and later to military school.

Upon graduation, my father's marriage was arranged by his mother and his spouse's parents, a common practice during my father's day. They had a son named Theodore. The story becomes cloudy here as to whether his wife reunited with a childhood love or he met my mother and had an affair, resulting in a divorce. One of the stories told by my mother is that my father's mother arranged for his ex-wife to marry someone else and requested that my father give Theodore up for adoption to his ex-wife's new husband. There was a lot of anger during this time, and my father was cast out from his family. This became the repeated pattern in my father's life; he would marry five times, each time assuming custody of the children, even when they were not his own. After one divorce, for instance, his step-daughter decided to live with him rather than with her mother or father.

After gathering this insight, I went to my father and showed him what I had discovered. Like most new students eager to use new knowledge, I gave him the diagnosis that we came from a "dysfunctional family." Of course the label baffled him, as his efforts over the years were all about keeping his children together and loved, trying to prevent the pain of separation he had incurred from happening to us. He even raised me as his own without whispering a word, just as he thought his son's adoptive father would have done for his son. He was like Joseph, trying to restore respect and honor to us as children, without having any familial support from his biological or adoptive families.

Now, several years later, I can see how we did receive love, and I have renamed what I once called "dysfunctional" as a negative love bond. Without exploring these family themes of adoption and rejection and their effects on us as children, I would not have uncovered the greater mystery of the God-Realization Genogram and the gifts of forgiveness, grace, and mercy. Regardless of these choices and the consequences, the Divine light within my siblings and me pressed forward to be known, to dissolve the crooked paths of our parents and ancestors, to bring the light forward, and to be healed. People reject people, but God loves us unconditionally and seeks our knowing His grace.

Each person in our family had to face the impulse of infidelity and master this pattern we were born into. The potential to repeat the pattern is interwoven into the very fabric of our being. We will either be faced with repeating the pattern ourselves or be in a relationship with a person who will betray us in the same way. Without self-knowledge and a deep understanding of your family tree, you can't hope to fully master the forces and restore the light within. This is the work people need to do prior to getting married. They must search for and discover these basic weaknesses, loss of grace, and negative love bonds so they can heal the past and come into full communion with each other. We must truly understand what we are born into and what our spiritual journey must be.

The first time I met my husband's family, I had an uncanny feeling that I didn't quite understand. When we left the meeting, I told my husband that his father had cheated on his mother. My husband looked surprised at first and then looked down sadly and said, "Yes, this is true." He had known since he was ten years old. His father had shared this information with him and betrayed his trust. My husband felt sad and angry that he knew. He was very young and felt betrayed by his father because he loved his mother, yet he had to keep his father's secret. Both of us had to look closely at these issues, at the adultery passed down in both our families, in order for our marriage to work. Otherwise, we would unconsciously repeat the same patterns.

Regardless of the infidelity, both my husband and I discovered the grace of God and found our spiritual roots. Even when unforgiveness from family members kept barriers and walls between people, God restored wholeness for each of us upon our asking. Working with the God-Realization Genogram empowered us to restore and claim the light within our family. God doesn't hold grudges; only people do. He gave his Son for us to understand that all sin is forgiven and we can be restored. All we have to do is ask.

The Healing Work

When uncovering and working towards healing infidelity within your family you may become overwhelmed by the hidden secrets, and unresolved consequences. Remember always ask God to be your guide. You can face and heal anything knowing that God is your Rock. I encourage you to move slowly and deliberately, step by step. You can use the God- Realization Genogram to help you identify any of the patterns and stay focused on your ultimate goal of restoration and healing. In addition you can start by looking within you and examining what is there along the lines outlined below. Once you understand all the forces that may be at work within you, your partner, and your families take your investigation outward and look at marriage and its physical aspects. Here's how you can begin.

The Heart of the Matter

Your heart is the center of all of your loving relationships. It regulates the flow of blood throughout every system of the body. It is highly sensitive to pain and betrayal and gives off signals to your brain and the rest of your body when you are in distress. If your heart is wounded, you must acknowledge the wound and what caused it. When our hearts are broken because of adultery, we lose faith in ourselves, our relationships, and the God within us. Actually, our whole world seems to crumble around us. Our dreams and ideals about our family start to dissolve into a sea of confusion, pain, and anger. The trust and faith we have built with our partner is shattered, and we are consumed by disillusionment. If the married couple has children, each child is affected differently, and their ideas, feelings, and thoughts about marriage change. The basis of trust and safety in their family are compromised by this very act.

Think about what it would take to heal this wound. Is an act of forgiveness in order? Is there anger to be released? Consider what needs to be done and how you might go about doing it. If the heart isn't healed, the wound will color everything we do or feel until it is right again. If you committed adultery, consider why you may have made this choice rather than respectfully asking for a divorce. Were you unhappy for years, or dealing with other problems, or repeating a family pattern? Regardless of the reason, remember you too are loved and this is part of your soul growth. You do need to make amends, help others heal, and take responsibility for your actions. You may have some good excuses for your behavior, yet blaming another for your dishonesty will never restore you. Only your self-honesty and search for the truth will set you free.

The Soul Enshrouded

For those of you who have committed adultery, imagine how it covers your soul. Or if you were betrayed by your partner, consider deeply how the issue came about. Regardless of whether you are the one who was betrayed or who had an extramarital affair, this process can help you to understand and free yourself from years of pain and anguish. Remember that when anyone commits adultery, they have already lost a sense of their own integrity and may be repeating a generational negative love bond. This may be helpful for both parties in lieu of all the pain and anguish that can impinge the heart and enshroud the soul.

Adultery can cover the very essence of your being and then you cannot experience your full potential in your marriage. If you were born into adultery like me, your light is still there, waiting for you to claim and restore it. Through understanding and forgiveness, your light has an opportunity to shine forth.

In today's world, there are ways in which to honorably close a relationship before starting another. Unfortunately, in these times, our impulses and vanity override integrity and Divine wisdom. In addition, try reflecting on your family as I did, and see if adultery from your parents or other ancestors is covering your soul while unconsciously guiding you into a generational negative love bond. You see, sometimes we are born into these patterns, unbeknownst to us. We adapt to our families and their perceptions of life without understanding what is happening. If adultery has been present in your family, you may be acting out of the unconscious energy and the negative love bond that wants to be healed.

For me to find my true self, to master these impulses, I needed to understand my family history. Adultery was exposed and hidden on both my mother's and father's sides of the family. It caused many rifts and other problems that sent my father into exile. It also created a pattern of adoption in both families that continues today. I was actually born into the seeds of adultery and it was interwoven throughout my very existence. This is and was my soul growth opportunity. Unraveling this mystery had led me back into the arms of God.

The Eyes and Clear Vision

When our eyes are aligned to the Divine within, we see the world and others with integrity. When we are misaligned, our eyes become blinded, and we see what we want to see. We start to look at the world and others from a place of self-betrayal and vanity. Our illusion is that we are seeing what we want to see and then rationalize why it is true. But once self-betrayal is set into play, the eyes can be blinded and not see the far-reaching consequences. We can't see that we are betraying ourselves, our spouse, the third party involved, our children, our relatives, our friends, or our coworkers; all are affected. We can be shortsighted about the financial costs, as well as the real and pertinent issues in the marital relationship. We cannot see how we disconnect from the Divine within us and from our partner, our children, our extended family, and our descendants. Our immediate need to satisfy our impulses overrides our integrity. I often wonder, if we had a viewfinder that would allow us to see the probable outcomes of each choice we make, would it actually be a deterrent? If we could see the effects on our children and family for generations, would we change our choices in that one moment? I invite you to pretend you do have such a viewfinder. Open your vision to see beyond the moment of impulse to what might come of your current choices. What do you see? What will you do differently? If you are considering adultery, can you see an alternative way to handle your unhappiness while still respecting your spouse or partner? Can you handle this impulse with integrity, or does the serpent have you by the tail? Are you actually addicted to the risk-taking behavior? Can you talk with God and find another way through this spiritual crisis?

Considering the Hands

Imagine the light within you joined with your spouse and your children. You are one body of light born out of the bosom of the Divine. Now, imagine sexually or sensually touching another person in the same way you touch your spouse. Notice how your life force moves away from the Divine within you and then away from your spouse and children. Notice how this affects your limbic system and bonding with your family on a primitive level. How does it make you feel inside? How does it affect your connection to your spouse and children? How does the experience of being *one body without shame* change? How much energy is needed to keep yourself split inside, betraying your own integrity?

Of course many of us do not understand this basic principle of becoming one body of light with our marital partner and how it is fundamental to our physical, psychological, interpersonal, and spiritual health and well-being. Out of our own misunderstanding and ignorance, we commit adultery and block the light within us. In Corinthians 12:12, Saint Paul teaches us that the members of the Church are parts of the one body of Christ. Each person and their gifts and talents are important to the wholeness or holiness of the Church. The light within each person is to be respected and nurtured as part of the whole. How do you nurture that light? What is that about for a couple, a marriage, and a family? What does it mean to be a family in one body of light or Christ Consciousness?

Before marriage, none of us are truly taught the meaning of bringing our light into union with our partners or how to maintain being one body of light. We may have an intellectual understanding and a few experiences of such connectedness, yet what manual or book guides us on a daily basis into union?

A Matter of Maintenance

This book isn't meant to be a relationship manual, and the topic of sexuality is too broad to cover here, but I would like to make a few points about maintaining a marriage, because healing the breaches of our ancestors might be found in how we live in our relationships every single day. You should know, for instance, that most marriages cycle around in four phases:

1. Attraction and Eros Phase: Peak Experience (The power of Love and Eros attracts two people together)
2. Plateau and Leveling off Phase: Learning about each other (Vices are uncovered, secrets shared, etc.)
3. Distraction and Fault Finding Phase (Energies and attention are pulled away from the partner, you see each other's faults, and you are pulled toward other things, not necessarily toward another person; the distraction could be due to jobs, children, everyday stress)
4. Circle Phase: Movement out of distraction and out of relationship, or back toward the relationship (to attraction again)

Couples that last a long time know how to negotiate this cycle. They know that most problems arise during the Distraction phase. They find different ways to weather the storms until they move back to attraction again.

In the Distraction and Fault-Finding Phase, sexuality often takes center stage, with one or both parties complaining that intercourse has become non-existent or boring, and they just go through the motions. They want to do something different, but they don't know how. Often one person will have an affair, thinking the sex will be better, but in reality, it's only about the newness. They're doing the same thing because they haven't grown sexually and sensually. They end up going around the cycle and becoming bored again in a few years.

Many of my clients note dissatisfaction in their sex lives with their partners long before the affair starts. Oftentimes, it is overshadowed by other stressors mentioned above. The *Miami Herald* recently reported that 70 percent of married couples don't have sex because of factors that include stress, children, and the fact that both partners work and have limited time together. In addition, couples claim they know a lot about making love to each other, yet each person reports disappointment that his or her sexual needs are not being met. Nevertheless, because they may be uneducated sexually, their egos would be wounded to think they are ineffective as a sexual partner, or they are afraid to explore new ideas. So, most couples continue to pretend while the sexual relationship disintegrates.

I find it helpful for couples to read and explore healthy books that teach sexual pleasure. A couple's bed is a place for them to learn how to relax, love, and find intimacy and pleasure with each other. The act of making love triggers serotonin and other chemicals that bathe the body with pleasurable feelings and relaxation. Intimacy through healthy, fun sex provides the basis for keeping a couple together. Just as babies do not thrive without touch, neither will a marriage or relationship that doesn't have intimacy, touch, and love. You may have a good friendship, yet is this truly marriage?

Talking about sex is difficult for many couples. Usually one person feels inadequate for failing to give the other person satisfaction. Both men and women become offended when told they are not great lovers. They feel that what they have always done has worked. Instead of trying to find better ways to please their partners, they shut down, get angry, and pout. This behavior can lead to an affair, where either the man or woman goes outside of the marriage to restore his or her feelings of intimacy or potency. They may use all the same methods as they did before with their new partner and find it works, but this can be misleading since the new relationship (as mentioned above) is still in the honeymoon phase and boredom hasn't entered it yet. Affection, physical touch, and intimacy need to be built upon and nurtured every day. If these are left to die on the vine, they may wilt entirely, and never be resuscitated.

Couples who enrich their sex lives by exploring their bodies as part of building a healthy relationship tend to have a better chance of staying together. I encourage couples to explore the sacredness of their sexuality in an open, healthy, non-threatening way. And for those of you who may be saying, "Hey wait a minute! I thought we had a great sex life and my partner still cheated!" the situation being played out can be very complicated and most likely relates to unresolved early childhood experiences and or generational roots.

Internet and Betrayal

The Internet has added a whole other level to the mix, with opportunities for online infidelity available at the touch of a keyboard or the click of a mouse. What's more, people engage in questionable behavior online but discount it, claiming it's not "real." Men especially tend to put it in the same category as looking at *Playboy,* thinking there is no harm done to their spouses. However, when it comes to online material, people become limbically bonded to the images on the computer or the person they're chatting with. The cords of consciousness that would connect with their partner are now going through the computer system, and they develop their sexuality through that. It becomes a drug and then it becomes a risk. They are addicted and inevitably start doing it at work risking their job. The addict starts sneaking around and doing things that create that erotic feeling they simply must act out. This type of addiction doesn't discriminate; it captures the life force of all cultures: men, women, young adults, rabbis and priests, business men and school teachers—just to name a few.

As soon as you start risking your relationship with your partner and your community, everything changes. And when it gets exposed, everything falls apart around you. In healing the situation, you have to come back to your connection to the Divine and come to grips with the destructive nature of what you're doing. We're talking here about adultery but looking at this word as a verb: adulterate. Doing this makes it easier to understand how we are damaging ourselves. To *adulterate* means to render something poorer in quality by adding another substance, typically an inferior one. It is akin to pollution. A person caught up in online sexuality adulterates their own Divinity within themselves before their spouse. The brain takes in certain information over and over, and it wants it again and again. It acts like a computer and stores these complex sexual desires into the deep limbic system. By nature we are wired to bond and procreate. When we add into the mix another person or pornography, the limbic system becomes stimulated with the new wiring. It replays the same wiring, wanting the rush from the risky behavior. This is why God wants us to be aware of how we can adulterate our own good and diminish our connection with the light in ourselves and our partners.

The people who get caught up in all this are good people. They just don't understand how delicate and important our mind-body connection is. It's programmed for the Divine, and when you program it for something else you lose these deeper connections. This is why God made this Commandment so important—because adultery fragments all the relationships that would make us all one body. It fragments our ability to create union, to feel that twinkle we see in our partners. We also have to remember that the Divine in us can never be destroyed, only fragmented and diffused. We're constantly looking to heal it, to bring it back together.

For some, it is right to end their marriage with integrity, so as to not to shame oneself or one's partner. In other cases, the adulterous act represents deep-seated issues that re-create a childhood trauma and feelings of inadequacy, shame, and guilt, which can be worked through with a specialist. Whatever your position, whether you are the wrongdoer or the wronged, whether the adultery is elsewhere on your family tree or you are helping a friend worked though this Key, it will help you to consider the following questions:

Seventh Commandment Reflections

1. If adultery has affected your life, your parents' lives, or your ancestors' lives, how have you coped with it?
2. Do you have any unresolved feelings or issues resulting from it?
3. What are your beliefs about adultery? How do these beliefs affect you today? Are they loving and kind or punitive?
4. If adultery was in your family tree, how did you or your family members handle the situation? Was it talked about? How did you or they express their pain? Did they suppress it and keep secrets? Did people act out in other ways?
5. Contemplate how adultery affects the person's sense of self-respect and respect for the other and God.
6. Does the extramarital affair mask something else missing in the person or in the relationship?
7. What does the person need to reorient their consciousness toward radiant grace, forgiveness, mercy, and healing?
8. Pray to open the "crooked way" within your or their consciousness for understanding the truth and the root issues that need healing and grace.

9. Pray for healing of any of your or their ancestors who were held in bondage by their fear and extramarital behavior. Write out your prayer and say it each day in order to free the generational negative love bond.

10. Pray for your children and future generations that everyone can be restored to God's grace and love. Write out your prayer for your children and future generations. Say this daily. Praying for our children and descendants sends blessings and support for a thousand generations.

The sacredness of oneness is God's message to us. Through marriage, you can become one with your partner. God calls us to heal our splits or sense of disconnection from the light within us so we can experience Divine union with our partner. All healthy marital relationships can emanate the Seven Divine qualities. I will mention the first three here and you can explore all seven in Chapter 15 of this book. The first, Divine Trust, requires us to trust in God, trust in our own light, before we trust in our partner or others. The second, Divine Self-Love and Self-Acceptance, requires that we awaken to God's love and acceptance for us, that we must give that love and acceptance to ourselves and our shortcomings before we can truly accept and love our partner. And the third, Divine Respect, requires us to understand the universal concept of God and all creation: respect for the Divine light within us and respect for the Divine light in our partners. These are three fundamental Divine qualities for the health and well-being of our life, our marriages, and our relationships with our children.

Adultery overshadows and disperses these Divine qualities. When we practice meditating on the Commandment in our hearts, souls, eyes, and hands, we master the forces that want to split our light away from our partners and families. The health and well-being arising from the Divine principle of *marriage without shame* can fully be expressed through us to our mates and to our families when we tame the unbridled impulses within us. Self-understanding, love, and commitment can help us to uncover our light and become whole. Our children and descendants are depending on us to free ourselves and become unified. Regardless of what we are born into, when we rectify and restore ourselves to wholeness, God promises us blessings from a thousand generations. Give yourself the opportunity to reclaim the light within and experience the feelings of oneness with your partner and children! Just imagine that your light can shine a hundredfold when united with your partner and transmitted to your children.

Chapter 12

The Eighth Commandment: The Key to Potential

You shall not steal. ~Exodus 20:15

When you think about the weightier matters of the previous Commandments, you could justifiably wonder: "Why does God care about something as petty as stealing? Aren't the other Keys, connecting us directly to God and the people we love, more important?" But to fully understand the Eighth Commandment, I encourage you here to really try to think as God thinks, not as humanity thinks. God knows that stealing disconnects you from the creative power of the Divine within you. When you steal, you lose connection with yourself first because you're writing off your ability to achieve and acquire things in your own right. Instead of focusing on your own power (through God) to get what you want, you steal it from someone else, and you are spiritually diminished as a result.

When you steal, you affirm your inability to achieve success based on a direct relationship with God and the abundant universe. You disconnect from the Divine within you and begin a kind of lying to yourself about what you can acquire for yourself in the material world. You lose all sense of trust in God for prosperity, and this misconception builds an unhealthy belief system that replaces the God-Realization Process for you.

We see this in children all the time. They act out of innocence and have no proof of what can be provided for them. In fact, the world has told them it can't provide. When I worked in a juvenile center in the 1980s, I met a lot of kids who got in trouble for stealing. Their explanations were almost always identical: "I wanted one for myself, and my parents couldn't get me one." Such a motive is a cross between innocence, ignorance, and desire. No one has taught them how to acquire things for themselves. They don't understand that they can mow a lawn down the street and save

111

their money to buy a bike. Even worse, if a parent gets them out of trouble, the kids don't have to take responsibility for their actions. Instead, they get a high from stealing.

I knew one boy who did just that. He had everything going for him, yet he got into the habit of stealing, breaking and entering, and was caught several times. He actually told me he got a rush from this behavior. It was like a high for him to steal and see how he could outsmart others. We all thought it was a phase and that he would eventually turn his life around. His parents struggled out of love, and his girlfriend stood by him, but the high was so great that he gave up several scholarships for college and took to the lifestyle of a thief. He lost his moral compass and was riding on a wave of addictive, compulsive behavior. Some kids who steal keep doing it, taking on more and more risk. They don't want to change their behavior because it is how they're bonded in the world, and they lose their connection with Spirit in the process. Other kids try stealing something, don't find the adrenaline rush comfortable, and stop many times before they get caught. Maybe it was a couple of beers or a few dollars from their mom's purse, but their moral compass kicked in, and the sense of real guilt overrode the impulse to steal.

The Power of Creation

God wants us to know we can create anything we want as long as we connect with the mind of God and take the steps to bring it into the world. Though "ask and you shall receive" is one of the parables, it also works in reverse; in other words, if you don't ask, you don't receive, and some people are too impatient to ask and wait to receive. They want to jump from Step 1 to Step 10 and not do the work in between. They don't understand it's a process. Writing a book like this, for instance, doesn't happen overnight. You have to work out all the ideas you want to convey, put the concepts down on paper, and then write and rewrite and rewrite again. Most people don't like the idea of all that work; they just want the book to show up completed. It's the same when someone gets an idea, but thinks they don't have to work and things will just manifest on their own. This mindset has created a lazy generation that doesn't want to work. They want their parents to give them fifty dollars the minute they ask for it. Why mow a lawn or get a job at the mall instead? Recently, I tuned into the Joyce Myers television show, and she was speaking about the same truth, that "God is vast and inclusive of all things in the universe. If you don't ask, you won't receive." I was moved by her presence and message, yet I could see there was much more to Joyce Myers than asking God. She is committed, dedicated, hardworking, and has put in the time to manifest her dream. She is a God-driven woman and gives 200 percent toward working for God. Our youth today need inspiring people like Joyce if they are to learn how to ask and work for their dreams.

With the Eighth Commandment, God lets us know, "Stealing takes you away from what I have to offer you. I have all these blessings. When you take someone else's blessings, you're not open to receiving your own. You're missing out on what your potential is in the world." Open your heart and deeply consider this. It's as simple as knowing that you have to dream of something you desire to work toward and create. Look at what others have created. Did it just magically appear for them? How much time did they put in to create it?

Of course you could argue that some people put just as much time into figuring out how to steal something. These days, stealing is practically an art form and happens in so many complex ways on many levels. There are complex systems set up to steal identities, elaborate Ponzi schemes reaping billions of stolen dollars for thieves such as Bernie Madoff, and unethical behavior by banks and corporations costing investors and taxpayers billions of their hard-earned dollars. How do we find relevance in this Spiritual Key today when it is breached on such a huge level?

That Which Is Taken

There are many stories in the Bible where we see instances of stealing. David sought to steal the affections of Bathsheba. Jacob sought to steal Esau's blessing. But I believe the story that best illustrates the essence of this Key is not one where someone stole; it was about the victim of stealing. How does it feel, and what does that feeling mean, when someone steals something from you? When someone takes something, it feels hurtful to the heart. If you're bonded with the stolen object (such as a car), you can even be physically sickened by the loss. It can even affect your connection with God.

Christ teaches that we must let it go. "If someone takes your cloak, do not stop him from taking your tunic" (Luke 6:28-30). That which has been taken will come back to you another way. It's about becoming unattached to things. Christ tells us it is not worthy of all that pain and suffering and that we must put our faith in the Divine. We are asked to love our enemies. "Then your reward will be great, and you will be the sons of the Most High (Luke 6:35)."

This is exactly what played out in the biblical story of Job. In a conversation between the devil and God, the devil argued, "You've blessed Job. He walks in your ways, and he's prospered greatly. If you took all that away, he would curse you. He wouldn't be praying to you and putting you first." It was basically the old challenge, "When I take something away from you, will you still love me?" Think of how many times you or someone you know has questioned God's love because of something bad happening. Did a tragedy or loss ever make you want to turn away from God? Job faced this challenge on a massive scale. He endured the loss of children, land, wealth, and health. He had that same human struggle with faith that is still played out every day. People told Job he was cursed and that God no longer loved him, but he refused to believe that. He remained true to God and to the Divinity within him. In the end, when Job persevered at last, everything was restored to him.

Everything was restored to Job because of his integrity and faith. We learn that Job wasn't attached to his belongings or family, regardless of the physical and psychological pain he endured. He understood one fundamental principle: that everything he has ultimately belonged to God. When faced with our own loss, pain, and suffering, we can learn from Job how to practice non-attachment and stay steadfast in our faith. Many times we stay attached to the things we have lost or that were stolen. And that's the illusion! We labor under the idea that *we* own things and accomplish things, but nothing really belongs to us. You can manifest more and more, but it doesn't really belong to you. You can use the resources you attain to bring joy and pleasure to your life, but if you're so attached to those things that they are first in your life, it's like the parable of a camel going through the eye of a needle. Your attachment will cover your light and not allow your true potential to manifest. The thing will have become an idol, and you will lose your faith in Spirit. Your whole spiritual life will go off track.

Stealing and the Limbic System

The human brain is programmed by generations of human experience. The experience of loss and devastation programs the deep limbic system for survival. We adapt to our surrounding experiences and our limbic system records the information in the hardwiring of the brain.

Chemically, the feeling of anxiety experienced during theft triggers our natural survival mechanism, which releases adrenaline and other endorphins, producing a physiological high. Once set in motion, this alternative behavior and the resulting stimuli replace the body's real needs. The receptor sites are reprogrammed to receive these alternative chemicals, and an addictive feeling associated with this sneaky, risky behavior becomes the norm. As stated before, I've known young people who were at the top of their classes at school or star athletes on their school teams, but all of a sudden they wanted to counterbalance all of the positive behavior by taking risks. They might steal something and feel a high because they had taken a risk and didn't get caught, but to do that they had to set aside their natural gifts and become bonded with this addictive high that only gets bigger and bigger until it takes over.

In other situations, the act of theft may be a passive-aggressive attempt to release tension or anger that can't be expressed directly, especially with people who suffer from post-traumatic stress. Those who suffer from compulsive addictions, such as alcoholism, drug, food, gambling, sex, stealing and financial infidelity, and so on have often suffered a traumatic event that relates to a loss sense of self, a disruption in their authentic need for others. Or the behavior becomes a habit to reduce stress or other negative feelings and thoughts. Regardless of the situation, the compulsive behavior suppresses the soul's authentic experience and relationship to God within around this particular issue. Most of these addictions are related to a loss of connection to God-Realization, where trust, self-love and self-acceptance, and respect were replaced by physical, emotional, mental, interpersonal, and spiritual deprivation. Oftentimes, any type of unhealed trauma can move a person towards an addiction. Trauma usually undergirds an addiction and causes disruption in the deep limbic system which modulates cravings, desires, emotions, and behaviors. In a negative love bond, the brain bonds love with the addictive behavior, and chemical imbalances replace healthy nurturance and God-Realization.

In any active addiction, the individual reorients their inner world to this gross lie without ever consciously understanding what is missing. The addictive behavior replaces the authentic need for security, trusting in God and others, love, acceptance, and self-respect, which are all precursors to enjoying healthy relationships and social ties to the community.

Unfortunately, addicts lie to the people they love. From a broader perspective, the addict feeds off of and abuses the love of others because their love for self is lost. This, in essence, is yet another form of stealing. Authentic love cannot reach the receptor sites because they are bogged down with the chemicals created by risk taking, deceit, and lying. The addictive substance, thought, or behavior becomes the *love object*. The person consciously and unconsciously becomes bonded to the replacement love object for survival, rather than bonding to authentic love from God and those around them.

The repetitive cycle of addiction is chronically frustrating, because the addict protects the replacement love object as if it were the authentic love object. The ignorance within this thought disorder infuriates everyone who loves the person. They don't understand how and why a person would prefer the replacement substance, behavior, or thought for real love. The addict protects and loves the replacement object in the same way that others want to be loved by them. But the attachment, the NLB, actually circumvents human relationships and love. And in its role as computer center, the brain doesn't distinguish between the authentic and inauthentic (replacement) love objects.

Feelings of guilt and shame create an internal sense of badness, which can automatically produce chemicals in the brain that signal sadness, depression, or inappropriate anger. Repetitive feelings of guilt and shame stimulate emotions that are easily bonded with inappropriate behaviors such as stealing. This cycle covers underlying feelings of worthlessness and failure. This repetitive behavior creates endorphins and other chemicals that are related to gratification and bonding. So an influx of these chemicals becomes tied to a negative behavior that circumvents the authentic gratification that comes from a deep sense of trust, love, and respect in knowing God's grace.

Everyday Stealing

Of course, not all stealing is as deep and complex as an addiction. Many people have stolen things when they were young. We have those impulses to eat a candy bar in the store or steal a shirt, but however minor the impulses, there are still side effects. How do you feel when you get ready to do something like that? You might feel anxious or overtaken by a sense of sneakiness and paranoia. Those feelings are telling you that you're out of order, but sometimes we have to try something before we can understand it's not for us. Some people come to the conclusion that all the feelings of anxiety and rushing adrenaline are not worth it, while others think the adrenaline makes them feel good. So, we have to go deeper and think about what is in our minds and in our hearts when the opportunity to steal presents itself.

A few years ago, my sister-in-law Maria and I were shopping at a Macy's post-holiday sale to buy discounted Christmas decorations. When we checked out, Maria was handed a bag of ornaments she didn't pay for; they belonged to someone else. We discovered the bag after we had walked out and started laughing. Though the ornaments were discounted and probably didn't cost more than a few dollars, we joked that it would be funny if she kept them and in the afterlife heard St. Anthony say, "Sorry. You can't get into the Pearly Gates because you kept those ornaments!" She decided to take them back, knowing that in the end, it's just not worth it.

How many times has this happened to you? How many times did you alert the cashier to a mistake? Of course, there are also times when you don't. Maybe you were in a bad mood that day or you thought, "I always do this, and it doesn't matter anyway." We tend to rationalize stealing. It's the same when you leave work and pick up some pens and pencils from the supply closet to take home. We think no one will notice, so it doesn't matter. Or maybe you walk past a gourmet plate set up for a party in a hotel common area and pick up something to eat even though you're not part of the party, claiming, "Oh, I couldn't help myself."

Do these small acts of thievery matter? It all comes down to what is in your mind and in your heart when you are going to do it. Does your pride come in? Do you feel entitled? Do you minimize it? As soon as you minimize it, you might feel that something has come out of you. Some people become numb to it because that's how they've learned to be in the world. They do this instead of figuring out how to create their own dream and steps to success. Is stealing taking you away from knowing, "I can create this on my own"? Is this the way you want to spend your energy?

Keeping It in the Family

Many families today constantly replay the Jacob and Esau story of the stealing of birthrights and blessings. A patriarch or matriarch dies, and suddenly the family falls apart in rancor over written wills and who gets what. One or more people decide that someone in the family isn't worthy, and many try to trick family members or blatantly steal from a trust fund. They go to court and try to take what they didn't get, what they think is rightfully theirs. Usually it's a person who feels entitled, someone who undermines the rest of the family in order to take everything without accountability, and then everything crumbles. What happens to the people who suffer the stealing? Can they find their own path through it? If we're talking about blessings from a thousand generations, these patterns can stay in a family for a long, long time.

Such conflicts have affected both my husband and me. Jeff suffered for over thirty-five years because he married outside of his heritage and had to give up his birthright blessing from his father. Likewise, my Grandfather Evans betrayed his grandfather's wishes and married my grandmother, who was of Russian descent, so his inheritance was given to his children. My father was adopted and then forced by his mother to give his first son up for adoption when he left his wife and married my mother. He became an outcast and never saw his adoptive mother and sister again.

If you feel compelled to enter this kind of disagreement or disruption in your family, I encourage you to look back over your Family Tree of Knowledge. Has this ever happened in your family before? Are you reliving a pattern that has been passed down through the generations? Can you see the effects of the pattern? Now the choice is yours: Do you want to continue this pattern of harm and disconnect? Will you have to let go of your attachment to something? What would you need to do to bring about a peaceful resolution?

The Healing Work

The sacredness of this Key is again revealed when you meditate on it within your heart, soul, eyes, and hands. You open yourself up by being honest and looking at how stealing has affected your life. You may start to look at any area where you have stolen something or explore how theft has affected your family. By exploring each aspect, you open yourself to God-Realization and reclaiming your light, your dreams, and your integrity. While meditating on this Key in your heart, you may ask how stealing has affected you personally. How has it affected your relationship with others? Have you felt betrayed when someone has stolen from you? Do you steal or hold grudges? Work with the Key to uncover and unravel the greater mystery of love and forgiveness in your heart. You may have to forgive yourself, your relatives, your ancestors, or others. Take time to clear your heart.

Next, explore the Key as it relates to your soul, your dreams, and reaching your potential. Has stealing in any way covered your soul's dreams? Has what others have done to you or stolen from you caused you pain? For people who have been abused, their self-esteem, drive, and innocence may feel as if it was stolen. Reclaim your relationship with God, your drive, and your innocence. Unravel the greater mystery of your soul and reveal your true potential.

Now move up into your eyes. How do you see the world? Are you looking for things you can take from others, or are you paranoid someone is trying to take something from you? Regardless of either situation, your eyes need to surrender this cone of perception and reconnect to the Divine within. Can you see your true potential? Can you see how much work you need to do in order to manifest your dream? Can you visualize your dreams coming true? Open your eyes to seeing the truth and clearing away anything that inhibits you from seeing from the Divine within you.

Last, meditate on the Key in your hands. How do your hands manifest your own dreams? Do your hands work toward creation, aligned with the Divine within you? Do your hands need cleansing? Use prayer, meditation, and forgiveness and surrender to open the light within your hands. Turn your work over to God, knowing that everything you create is inspired by the mind of God and in the end truly belongs to our Creator. Allow yourself to become one with God and create your dreams. Allow God to work through you. You might find that your dreams manifest effortlessly when you surrender.

On another note, notice when you are in the creative wave with God and when you are not. How have all of these processes affected your brain? Have they moved you toward or away from your Divine center and integrity?

To be in creative flow, try to achieve the following:

- You trust in God.
- You love and accept yourself for your shortcomings.
- You respect the Divine within you.
- You relate to others and create with others from the Divine within them.
- You communicate your dreams by being centered within the Divine.
- You see or visualize your dreams and the steps toward manifestation.
- You know without a doubt that you are part of the Divine mind of God.
- You trust in your Divine potential.

Remember, to steal from others, one must be

- Disconnected from trust
- Feeling loss of self-love and acceptance
- Having disrespect for self and others
- Experiencing a loss of self-esteem or identity
- Unable to see others as helping you
- Unable to clearly communicate your dreams
- Unable to see your dreams come true
- Disconnected from knowing your Divine potential

Once you have completed this examination of where you are now, I invite you to look at your past behavior, using the following questions. You may write the answers in your journal or companion workbook.

Eighth Commandment Reflections

1. Contemplate your life. Did you ever steal anything in childhood or adulthood? If so, what was it?
2. What was happening in your life around the time you decided to steal something? Was it impulsive or premeditated? Describe the details.
3. Have you ever received something at the expense of another person's mistake? Did you correct the mistake or feel it was their loss, your gain? What thoughts, rationalizations, entitlement, guilt, or shame did you adopt to cover this action?
4. Do you still criticize or judge yourself for stealing? How does this relate to your sense of self and relationship with God?
5. Again, balance yourself with the *I AM* Meditation. Pray and meditate on each situation for more insight and understanding.
6. What do you need in order to heal and release yourself from these feelings? Do you need to pay someone back? Or do you need to do a good deed today as an active action, with God's grace, to restore your personal integrity?
7. Pray and ask God to help you with self-forgiveness and release of pain around your real guilt. Write out your prayer so you can repeat it as needed.

Next, here's a challenge for you. I invite you to regain faith in your own potential by going after something you want. Start by choosing something you want to achieve. Do a little research and find someone else who has achieved a similar goal. Write out the steps of what that person did to achieve the goal. Set up a schedule for yourself and give yourself time each day to fulfill one of those steps. Notice if any self-defeating thoughts come up. A lot of times, we find that when we try to do something, we have thoughts like, "It's too hard. You're never going to make it turn up." You have to change these negative, self-defeating thinking patterns from the negative to the positive. You can start by thinking, "What can I do today to reinforce the positive?" Maybe you can find out if your model person dealt with the same thoughts and doubts and look at the qualities they possess that helped them through it. Ask yourself, "How do I find those qualities within me?"

The beauty of this strategy is that the qualities you'll find are in fact Divine qualities. That means we all have those qualities. You may not feel them, but they are there. They're just lying dormant. Search out your Divine qualities. Feel the power of your potential. Once you feel the grace and strength of this connection with the Divine, you'll find that you can manifest what you want—only with the detachment that allows you to not fear it being stolen from you.

Chapter 13

The Ninth Commandment: The Key to Ourselves

You shall not bear false witness. ~Exodus 20:16

The LORD shall judge the people: judge me, O LORD, according to my righteousness and according to mine integrity that is in me. ~Psalms 7:8

What does it mean to lie? What exactly is the truth? The answers to these questions are never clear because words have many layers and many meanings. Add on to that the complexity of what is in our heads and our hearts when words are spoken, and you'll see how complicated the Ninth Commandment can be. To avoid bearing false witness, we must not lie about someone else. We must make a choice not to gossip or place responsibility or blame where it doesn't belong. While this is true, we deceive ourselves if we think on the surface: that we are keeping this Commandment as long as we're not hurting others. Most of the "bearing false witness" that we do starts from within, with the lies we tell ourselves.

In order to bear false witness, we compromise our integrity by first lying to God within and then lying to ourselves. This act covers the light within us and grows until we are lying to others. After that, we begin to change. We compromise our integrity and reorient ourselves to untruth. Our eyes will see the world from a place of deception and alertness in order to defend the lie. The process continues to grow until the liar projects their loss of integrity, grief, and sadness onto another. This sets up a karmic bond where the consequences of the liar are tenfold, since the recipient of the untruth now has to bear the unresolved karma of the liar. The liar has to live with the lies and the story around the lies, and this acts almost like a dark cloud of energy that tries to inhibit the light of the person. This truly is a painful process, as the dark energy covers the heart and soul of the liar with an unconscious shroud of despair and forgetting.

I believe the pain is profound because, if you disregard or break the Ninth Commandment, you are also in some way breaking all eight of the Keys that come before it. Remember that the focus of the Commandments go from God to self to family to your relationships with others and the world. Your integrity comes from being in alignment with the earlier Commandments. When you bear false witness, it is as if you've fallen through a funnel or vortex where you will ultimately dishonor all of these connections. You disrupt your direct connection with God within you.

I invite you to think about what happens in situations involving addiction. It's a good illustration of how the dangers of a lie can build upon themselves. If you're a family member of the addict, you likely think the addict's constant lies are a big problem. Most of the hurt and anger in a family crisis stem from the addict treating family members in painful, unloving ways. But the big problem started way back when the addict first indulged in the unhealthy action that became an addiction. First they had to lie to themselves in a way that allowed them to do it. They said, "I can handle it" or "This isn't so bad" or "I'll do it just this once." They probably said these things to themselves multiple times as the addiction developed, so by the time they reach full-blown addiction, they have been lying to themselves a lot longer than they've been lying to family members. They assure themselves that, "If I drink or take this, my problems or pain won't seem so bad. I can forget everything when I am high. I don't have to deal with my feelings if I eat something. It doesn't really hurt so bad." The initial lie can cover a hidden secret, pain, or sorrow from childhood, a time when the soul of the person was disrespected. A child doesn't have the proper coping mechanisms to deal with abuse or trauma and many times adapts to the situation and loses connection to the natural Divine light within. In quite the same way, young military men and women who suffer from post-traumatic stress can lose their sense of self and their integrity. They may engage in substance abuse to suppress and cope with the traumatic emotional effects of war, which we've already discussed. Combat may have required them to do something counterintuitive to their own integrity, and in the process, they may have lost their faith in God, their internal sense of light, and the light in others.

Lying is an important factor, and it sets up a disconnection. As soon you go out of alignment with your connection to God, the process of lying to yourself has already begun. Many crisis situations start this way. For instance a married man thinks about getting a card for another woman (not his wife). He feels anxious, ashamed and embarrassed, yet he continues to shop and buys her the card anyway. He knows immediately that he is out of integrity. His feelings are the result of God letting him know he is not in right order with his integrity, yet he begins to rationalize how "harmless" it is. Once he does so, he has begun to create that crooked path that can separate him from his wife and move him closer and closer to committing adultery. This is, as they say, a slippery slope. Fortunately for this man, he witnessed his anxious behavior, and was able to overcome his impulses, talk with his wife, and work through the feelings that were stimulated in relation to this other woman.

The Lie's Greater Effects

When you think of how lightly we take lying in today's world, it's hard to imagine that in the days of Moses, bearing false witness against another person might have resulted in that person being stoned to death. Back then, lying about another person could also lead to shaming, public humiliation, being stripped of possessions, or exile. On the spiritual level, lying about others creates separation and blindness from the universal truth of God's unending love, compassion, mercy, and understanding. Lying actually puts a twist, a "crooked way" into our relationship with the Divine.

As I mentioned earlier, lying plants the seeds of separation and crookedness that will eventually be transmitted to our family members. Although they may not be immediately apparent, the consequences of lying can be tenfold for one's descendants. Lying creates a parallel process that operates from fear but provides immediate gratification for egocentric needs. It also reconfigures the brain so that deceit, cunningness, and negative pleasure trigger the production of endorphins. Deception sets up a physiological template of addiction. Yes, a person can become addicted to the act of lying—thus the compulsive liar. The behavior reorients the mind and the chemical brain, from experiencing Divine luminous wisdom, bliss, and pleasure to lying, cheating, shaming, and negative pleasure.

If this continues, the brain eventually becomes wired to push away love. For instance, I have met several people who brush away a positive comment and will replace it with a negative statement of disbelief or self-criticism. Somehow, the brain wires love and criticism together, creating a negative love bond (NLB). Many of us are actually programmed to take in criticism rather than positive statements. The neurotransmitters in the brain become addicted to the chemicals produced by the criticism and self-hate rather than love and acceptance. A person's ability to respect themselves with humble self-love has been redirected toward self-hate and judgment. This false belief usually pairs love with criticism or rejection. In the subconscious, to be loved actually means to be criticized or rejected. The physical pleasure center of the brain doesn't recognize the difference. Whenever I ask such a person to slow down and take in the loving comments, they act surprised, shocked, embarrassed, and bashful. Yet, when they open themselves to receiving positive love rather than rejecting it, their body and face seem to relax, and an authentic smile appears. In one moment of slowing down, they can reorient their experience and change the *molecules of emotion*, as author Candace Pert calls them, within the brain. In this one moment, a person can actually repair and reprogram the brain to receive love and acceptance.

An Indication of Mastery

The lamp of the Lord searches the spirit of man; it searches out his inmost being. ~Proverbs 20:27

We see one of the first instances of bearing false witness in the Bible, after Adam and Eve had eaten from the forbidden tree and God asked who had told them they could do it. Adam immediately blamed Eve, and Eve blamed the snake. In this very first story of the Bible, the blame game had already started. No one would take responsibility. Eve did not take responsibility for mastering her own impulses and instead chose to bear false witness. The lie indicated where she was lacking, where she had not mastered the serpent or unbridled energy within her. Adam, too, deferred his own personal power and choices by blaming Eve. Hadn't God given him power over everything in the Garden—even Eve? Was it easier to blame her rather than take responsibility for his choice?

The same thing happened when Peter, who was accosted by the people after Christ's arrest, denied Christ three times. When there's a lynch mob coming for us, we are quick to bear false witness. Peter's fear made him do it—but he was forgiven. The forgiveness almost made him feel even worse, because Peter realized his fear was a part of himself that he didn't have mastery over. Christ recognized Peter's shortcomings. The question was, what would Peter do to rectify this, to develop mastery over his fear?

There are similar situations in the world today. Bad situations make people deny themselves. In the business world, when large corporations take a big fall, the truth is that many people within the company have known about it well in advance, but they were too scared to tell the truth. When a crime is committed and witnesses are asked if they saw anything, they often answer, "No, I didn't see anything." Why? Fear of retribution or death. Again, this is a lack of mastery over our fear. The lie actually reveals where the person lost their faith and trust in God.

Our hidden fears can run amuck, causing us to act impulsively and lose our Divine connection. I learned this lesson twenty years ago while attending a weekend workshop. During one of the breaks, everyone was walking down to the water to hang out and share. While I was walking toward the water with some friends, I heard an inner voice that said, "Donna, you need to walk on this path into the woods." Surprised, I actually replied, "Gee, I would like to just go hang out with friends."

Nevertheless, the voice seemed adamant, so I took off on my own into the woods. As I was walking, I could hear a rustling sound. At first, I was just curious about why I was in the woods and not with my friends. I ventured deeper into the woods via the path, and while I was walking, the noises became more distinct. I could feel myself becoming anxious and afraid. I started to think someone was following me or there was some large animal in the woods. With each new sound, I became startled. Then, I heard the voice again, "Donna, you are scared of the wind!"

I stood there for a moment and realized how true the statement was. I was filled with fear and could project my fear onto anything, no matter how trivial or ridiculous. If the mere wind could scare me, where else in my life was I operating from fear? Needless to say, this experience changed my life. I discovered that my unbridled fear had the best of me and that I was listening to fear rather than God. This is how we start to lie to ourselves. Instead of standing on the rock of God when we become afraid, our fight-or-flight mechanism attaches itself to superfluous events, causing an undue amount of fear, anxiety, and depression. Fear and lying go hand in hand, and both need to be mastered. They undergird bearing false witness.

Bearing False Witness Within the Family

God says that when we bear false witness, we disrupt something in the very fabric of our relationship with the Divine. It sets up a karmic current within the people involved so that we live with that lie later. I once met a young man who shared with me the story of breaking up with his girlfriend, with whom he'd had a child. He was planning to marry her but didn't know she had fallen in love with a friend of his. He was, however, noticing some strange behavior from her: She would make a point of leaving him alone with his daughter. For instance, while he was showering, she would, without warning, thrust the baby into the shower and make him take her. He eventually learned she was preparing a custody battle and was trying to set him up for accusations of child sexual abuse. He had to fight the massive web of lies that were engulfing him if he was going to maintain custody of his child.

By bearing false witness against her child's father, the mother had created a rift in the family, a disconnection with Spirit. It was likely she thought she could get away with it and her child would be none the wiser, but the karmic effects have already begun. The little girl in this story is growing up amidst all these lies her mother created against her father so that her mother could gain sole custody. Even though we think that young children will never know the truth, it will inevitably come out one day. My father didn't think I would ever learn he was not my biological father, but he couldn't keep it hidden from me forever. Just like this little girl, secrets affect children for the whole of their lives.

Family Lies and Deception

Whenever a family member disregards one or more of the Commandments, the spiral effect of lying occurs within the family mind field. The lie becomes buried deep beneath the surface, and the person and family adopt many behaviors to cover the lie. Unfortunately for the family, these lies become deeply ingrained in the family system. Some of them are adopted as false truths and seem crazy from an objective witness's perspective. Lies that are passed down generationally are difficult to uncover without compassionate reflection, prayer, meditation, and exploration into the maladaptive patterns and negative love bonds within the family system. The long-term effects can be seen by the unhealthy behaviors of one or more family members. If we become archeologists and excavate some of our old family material, these patterns on the God-Realization Genogram can reveal themselves as directly related to a breach in one of the Ten Commandments.

A false witness will not go unpunished, and he that pours out lies will not go free. ~Proverbs 19:5

When the person telling the lie is in a position of power—such as a teacher, a coach, or a business executive—the effects of that lie can go way beyond the family circle. Let's look at an example where the person in question held the highest office in the land: President of the United States. When Bill Clinton bore false witness against himself and declared, "I did not have sex with that woman," he used semantics to rationalize himself out of trouble. He didn't truly understand what he put into play for young people across the country: the President saying publicly that oral sex was not "real" sex. Many teenagers picked up on this because teenagers are impressionable. Many thought, "If President Clinton says it's okay, it must be okay." Right after the Monica Lewinsky affair, so-called "lipstick parties" became popular among teens, essentially a group of kids getting together in one room so the girls could perform oral sex on the boys. How outrageous! Mr. Clinton didn't realize how far reaching his lie would be because of his influence, and what it would cost. He had no idea of the severity of his nonchalance, so he took no responsibility for a lie that affected the lives of many of America's young boys and girls.

Little White Lies

This kind of discussion, by nature, must include "little white lies." Many people jump to questions such as, "Well, what if my aunt is wearing a terrible hat and she asks me if it looks good? Do I tell her?" These situations come up constantly, sometimes several times a day. How do you handle them? First, ask yourself, "Does it take something away from you or the person involved for you to tell the truth?" Is your aunt feeling really fabulous about that hat, and do you know it would depress her to say it's horrible? Would it make you feel bad to tell this truth? People can use truth to hurt and punish, and truth is no longer in the service of higher good if it's used to harm someone. Some people are all about speaking their truth, even if they knowingly hurt someone. Consider this when you are confronted with gossiping or examples of truth-telling in the media.

Can you turn around a situation so it mirrors the light in someone and helps that person take responsibility for their actions? Maybe telling the truth can help prevent them from further embarrassment. When you behave this way, it doesn't set into play all the other rippling effects and distortion. If you don't, who will set it right four or five generations from now? These are important concepts to reflect upon and consider.

The Healing Work

It could very well be that you are that person who must set things straight after four or five generations. Where do you start? You can begin by praying for more insight. First, look at yourself and determine whether or not you are breaching this Commandment in your own life. How did you learn to do that? Who taught you to place blame and not take responsibility? Are there stories about certain people (scapegoating) in the family? Is there truth here? Really look for and widen your cone of perception to include each person, especially the person who was ostracized. Maybe there's alcoholism in the family and everyone is caught up in what the alcoholic (we'll call him Joe) is doing to the family now, but no one is asking what happened before he became an alcoholic. Was he in a war? Did he lose a job? Are there hidden secrets, unbearable truths untold? You might find you have one part of a story, but not another. Did that happen because Joe's father behaved in a certain way? Does alcoholism or depression run in families that have experienced deprivation and trauma? Perhaps you need to change your cone of perception and look at the story from that person's viewpoint. Is that viewpoint represented in the family considerations? Many times it's not.

In my own God-Realization Genogram, I discovered an abundance of lies, deceit, and cover-ups that occurred when, out of fear and greed, my ancestors kept secrets, disowned people, and told lies for their own benefit. My father hid the truth from me for many years because he thought it was a loving thing to do. Others lied and tried to annihilate our family for other reasons, such as hate and greed. What they didn't know was that God would be pressing forward in me—regardless of the situation I was born into—to know the truth. God wants us to be whole and holy, regardless of the circumstances surrounding our birth. God is seeking for us to return to the Garden of Eden. People can try to destroy people, yet God's undying love for us presses forward. How has God pressed forward in you?

Ninth Commandment Reflections

I invite you to consider the following questions and write the answers in your journal:

Part 1

1. Have you ever told a lie about someone else? Explain. What was your personal gain?
2. What were the consequences for the other person? Were they hurt mentally, emotionally, physically, financially, or other?
3. Identify any addictive patterns repeated through your family: alcohol, drugs, adultery, and divorce.
4. Identify the underlying lie(s) or perceived causes to the problem.
5. Identify breaches in any of the other Ten Commandments.
6. Meditate on each of the Commandments in your heart, soul, eyes, and hands. How is each of these areas affected by the breach of bearing false witness? Are other Commandments broken? How? Pray with each Commandment until each area is clear and illuminating the true light within you.

Part 2

1. Using the information you gathered in the previous exercise, set aside time to meditate and pray to receive guidance and healing.
2. Use the *I AM* Meditation in Chapter 15 to clear your mind, body, and spirit.
3. Communicate with God and ask for what you need to restore yourself to wholeness and release this pattern. Notice how this situation affects you physically, psychologically, and spiritually. Open yourself up to receiving healing and ask for blessings. Let the Divine mind of God communicate with you. Keep a journal about your experience. Refer to Chapter 15 for other self-healing meditations and techniques.

4. What do you need to change for you? How do you plan to make those changes? Write out your plan. This will help you stay on track and go deeper in your personal journey.

Part 3

1. From the previous information, identify and make a list of others in your family who were affected, both alive and deceased. You can use the God-Realization Genogram to record your information. What challenges did they face or are they facing today? Depression, isolation, substance abuse, or others?
2. Set aside time to pray for each person on your list. Ask that you receive more insight and that each person be forgiven and restored. If there was a breach of a Commandment by a particular person, pray for them, that their soul will find God and inner peace.
3. Identify any areas where you have either consciously or unconsciously colluded with this pattern, these negative love bonds, and take time to pray for healing.
4. Refer to Chapter 15. Use the *I AM* Meditation to balance your mind, body, and spirit. Remember that you may need to go back and forth between the positive and negative experiences, emotions, and thoughts to help the deep limbic system change your negative love bond and to receive insight, restoration, and healing. What is your experience?

Although you may have uncovered areas of your life that need restoring and healing, remember that God gave us this Key to open the light within us. You have the opportunity to heal generations of pain and suffering caused by lies and to restore your true birthright, Divine oneness. It can be done simply by expanding your cone of perception and meditating on the Keys to open the light within your heart, soul, eyes, and hands. In this way, you can master the forces inside that try to deter you. You can overcome anything you were born into because this was God's plan even before you were born. Begin the process with hope and faith, knowing that God has watched over you all along, calling you toward the light! Bear witness to your light! Be free and at peace!

Chapter 14

The Tenth Commandment: The Key to Manifestation

You shall not covet.~ Exodus 20:17

You shall not covet your neighbor's wife. You shall not set your desire on your neighbor's house or land, his manservant or maidservant, his ox or donkey, or anything that belongs to your neighbor. ~ Deuteronomy 5:21

We all know the old saying, "the grass is greener on the other side." When we look at what others have, it sometimes seems they are getting the better deal, and this sows the seeds for constant dissatisfaction within our lives. The Tenth Commandment instructs us not to covet. On the surface, this sentiment may seem negative in a finger-wagging, be-happy-with-what-you-have kind of way, but there's so much more to it. The sacredness of being in tune with God's creative powers and our ability to manifest anything in our life is the key to mastering the desire to covet. When we desire and covet what belongs to others—whether it is success, power, or material wealth—we inhibit or block our ability to manifest our own desires.

Just as the first four Commandments refer to our personal relationship with God, and the Fifth and Sixth relate to understanding the importance of your heritage and family tree, this Commandment relates to our relationship with others and our ability to manifest what we want in life. Each Commandment builds upon the others and opens us to live fully from the light within. You can see how our relationship with God builds an internal sense of self and is the foundation for creating healthy, loving relationships.

Why does God state this Commandment last, after teaching us to love our neighbor as ourselves, as taught in Commandments Seven through Nine? I believe it is because God wants us to know how our desires and longings need to be focused on God first. Our desires, when focused on others, can lead us astray, away from reaching our true potential. Just as Christ tells us, "Love your neighbor as yourselves," we need to learn how to bring our light and creativity into the world. Respecting our own gifts and talents allows us to respect and encourage the gifts in others, but God specifies that coveting the gifts, talents, and material success of others will impair our ability to manifest our own. It will also lead us away from being in right relationship with the light within us. As a result, we start to fall from grace and possibly go on to break other Commandments.

Of course for many of us, it's hard not to admire or desire someone else's success, clothes, jewelry, material belongings, spouse, or children. Sometimes we even criticize ourselves, our spouses, or our children and see them as lacking because of what others have created or done. We may know and agree that this is coveting, but I don't believe we understand how coveting can produce jealousy, blame, depression, and eventually an internal disconnect from God's grace and blessings. We can become more outwardly focused than inwardly focused. Refocusing our intention toward our relationship to God opens us to blessings and releases us from negative consequences, while coveting another person's property or success blocks our ability to trust in our own success or prosperity, derived from communing with God.

Divine Potential

When we disregard the Tenth Commandment, we become bonded to what others have rather than to what we can create ourselves. We may become jealous, depressed, angry, or resentful. However, on a positive note, there is the possibility that when we see what others have, it may inspire us to live up to our Divine potential. It depends on how well we master the impulse when covetous feelings arise.

When we covet, our hearts, souls, eyes, and hands are redirected from the Divine within to the outer world. Our hearts can be covered by jealousy or resentment. Our souls' longing and potential can be covered by false desires. Our eyes might look at the world from a limited perspective, while our hands either become idle or reach for others' success rather than our own. We are born with a desire to live and thrive, and our desire is what we have to master. This Key is about our natural propensity to desire and create what we want in life. We first see it in the Garden of Eden, when Adam and Eve are told they can't have the fruit of the tree; that only makes them want it all the more. Desire was already there in the beginning. We desire knowledge and material goods. I think God is telling us that we need some self-mastery, or we won't know how to use our desire in a healthy, creative way.

I have a client who recently had an opportunity to send her young son to a private school on a scholarship. As she drove him to the school daily, she began to notice the cars of the other parents. One car in particular caught her eye: a chocolate brown Lexus RX-350. At first, she only thought the car was pretty and its color unusual. As she continued to see the car twice a day for several weeks, however, she began to feel that she wanted one, despite being unable to afford it. Fortunately, because of the work we had done together, she was able to recognize that what she was feeling was really covetous, and the coveting developed solely because she saw the car every day. Her desire had been activated by the repeated encounters with the object of her desire.

By making that simple acknowledgement, my client was able to begin demagnetizing her desire for the expensive brown car. While some people would have just gone out and bought something for themselves—maybe even a new car—to feel better about it, my client instead took steps to master the impulse. She stepped back so she could witness her thoughts and say, "I am doing this. I am coveting." She could then ask, "Why am I doing this?" and "Can I really afford it?" Through this questioning process, she was able to disconnect herself from desiring the car. I'm not saying that all of our desires are bad, but it is good to be able to question and understand them before we act on them.

Now let's look at how coveting operates in a different way. I know a man who makes negative comments every time he sees a person driving an expensive car. "Who does he think he is?" or "I bet he thinks the law doesn't apply to him!" He immediately assumes the person is rich and begins to minimize what he sees as their life and choices, even though he's not in a position to know anything about them. Maybe that person isn't even rich and is struggling to pay for the car. This man can, however, know himself by asking some pertinent questions: "Am I jealous? Why am I minimizing this person's life? What do I really want that is not in my life? Is this my way of acting out because I don't have what I want?"

This last question is especially important, because we often do things from a place of insecurity. We have a tendency to place ourselves in society. You might ask yourself, Where do I fit in this group of people? How much do I make? What have I accomplished? We make a lot of assumptions based on appearance and feel insecure when we think we don't measure up.

When you're connected to the Divinity within you, you know you can trust God to bring forth in you the life you want. You have the potential to create what you want in life, but here's the caveat: You must be willing to put in the work. Some people desire much, but they're not willing to put in the time to get it.

In the book *Outliers,* Malcolm Gladwell points out that most successful people put in 10,000 hours of work on their talent; they have a healthy positive addiction. In one example, he describes how Microsoft founder Bill Gates had the opportunity to indulge in his computer interests and put in his 10,000 hours at a very young age. He also had amazing technical understanding. He was born with that understanding, along with a drive and desire that made him willing to put in the time.

I have witnessed this in my son, who does a comedy routine while escaping from a straitjacket. He has worked on this piece since fifth grade. (As of this writing, he is a recent high school graduate.) In the beginning, he focused mainly on getting out of the straitjacket, but now he performs a whole routine in an entertaining, believable, and funny way. It took him a lot of time to perfect it to the point where he was actually performing. Success comes from a desire to know more and a drive to keep on keeping on. Napoleon Hill discusses this in his book, *Think and Grow Rich.* It is all about failure and drive. He talks about how Henry Ford put the time into building the automobile. Ford and many of the other successful people that Hill interviewed for the story talked about how much time and energy successful people put into something and how they dealt with failure. Ford would say, "I'm six steps closer to success" rather than "I failed." Most people quit right before they succeed. They hit one more obstacle, get worn down, and go into a self-defeating mode. Just think what might be accomplished if they all tried and tried again!

I think that some people have a desire but don't know how to follow it through from beginning to end. They want to go from Step 1 to Step 10 in one fell swoop, not realizing they have to take mini-steps in between. They must learn how to marshal their energy. There are different levels in energy and drive, but the unbridled energy is usually what moves us to do things. In some children or adults, it is focused and directed; these folks seem to get more done than the average person. In others, that force has to be directed and redirected, as though they were on a constantly curving path toward what they want.

Mastering Desire and the Light within Us

> *The Lord says to Cain: "Why are you distressed and why is your face fallen? Surely if you do right there is uplift. But if you do not do right, sin crouches at your door; its urge is toward you, yet you can be the master of it." ~ Genesis 4:6-7, The Mitzvah Torah*

Many of our biblical ancestors struggled with mastering their desires. So many stories in the Bible illustrate how coveting and desire are a basis for disconnecting from our Divine center. The serpent in the Garden of Eden represents the life force rising within us. Left untamed, it can lead us astray and cause suffering. But if mastered, it can lead us back to the Garden and into oneness with our Creator, creating blessings, prosperity, happiness, and health.

Coveting is a direct response to insecurity in our relationship with God and our inability to master our desires. We lose our connection to God's calling, to that still, small voice deep inside. Through our connection with God, everything can happen. If we put our time and energy in and focus, we can succeed. Some people never learn this and continue to blame others for their failures or faults. In the story of Cain and Abel, God teaches us how Cain's jealousy of Abel for winning God's favor and blessings evoked feelings of hatred and murderous rage. Cain lost his sense of self and connection to God's grace, love, and compassion. His inability to regulate his own feelings and thoughts triggered the irresponsible act of killing his brother, even after God had directly given Cain the secret to self-mastery.

Unfortunately, Cain never really understood why his grain offering was considered inferior to Abel's livestock sacrifice. The story illustrates that Cain was disrespectful by not offering God his first fruits, the best of his harvest. He put his own needs before God. Once God showed disapproval, Cain could not tolerate his own feelings of anger, jealousy, and competition, all of which made him feel unloved. Even though God told Cain that he would bear responsibility for contemplating his acts of sin, Cain refused to pray for understanding and instead acted impulsively on his feelings. He wanted his brother's blessing without having to pay the price of listening to and following God's instructions on how to master his own consciousness and respect the God within him.

Likewise, Jacob's desire for his brother's position caused him to flee and not fulfill his destiny until much later, when he met the angel. It wasn't until then that he was able to come back and heal his relationship with his brother.

Moses and Christ, both tempted by their desires, found ways to master their human impulses and better communicate with God. Moses struggled with his self-doubt about his speech impediment. Regardless of his worries, he was asked to confront the Pharaoh, free his people, and lead them to the Promised Land. Moses overcame his self-doubt and brought God's covenant to his people. Christ went to the desert, a barren place, to master temptation and the serpent within. He was able to tame this unbridled energy and focus his desires on God and fulfilling His potential.

Coveting in the Family

> *What shall we say, then? Is the law sin? Certainly not! Indeed I would not have known what sin was except through the law. For I would not have known what coveting really was if the law had not said, "Do not covet." ~Romans 7:7*

It seems to me that most coveting issues for families today center around inheritances. Perhaps it's because so many baby boomers are now coming into their family inheritances, but these issues are definitely front and center. I've seen behavior such as long-term plots to take another's inheritance, and sadly, the participants don't realize how this behavior limits their creative power to create more.

My husband Jeff experienced great difficulties in his family when his cousin's husband coveted his inheritance or portion of his father's and uncle's business. Jeff's behavior in his 20's played an important role in setting the stage for the takeover. As a young man in his rebellious years, he had married a Las Vegas dancer, and this affected his position in the family business. As the firstborn Jewish son—like Esau—Jeff was to be blessed with the leadership role. But his father was angry and, assuming that Jeff at the age of 21 couldn't make good decisions in his private life, he decided to punish Jeff at work. This set the stage for the next 30 years of working in the family business. Like many of us, Jeff at 21 didn't foresee the future consequences of his actions. He knew that his father had numerous adulterous affairs, but that behavior was acceptable if overlooked. Jeff's father continued to act out his disapproval by punishing Jeff at work.

Then his father and uncle made a decision that would change the course of Jeff's career in the family business: they hired his brother's firstborn-daughter's husband as president of the company. Unfortunately, under these circumstances it was an action that would have a lifelong effect on Jeff, his father, and his siblings. Over several years, Jeff's cousin undermined him, no matter what Jeff did. He blew up Jeff's mistakes and made a big deal of them in front of others. Regardless of whether his cousin lost large sums of money in the business or not, the negative focus was always on Jeff. It became an Esau and Jacob story.

This situation, with the same family dynamics, played out over thirty years. When his cousin couldn't convince Jeff's father to give him his stock after he retired, another plan unfolded: he covertly tried to squeeze the whole family out, until Jeff finally stood up and confronted the situation. He said, "I'm not going to stand by and watch you take it. If you want it, buy us out." The family dynamics, twists, and turns go much deeper, and everyone involved has their own perception. Yet in the end, Jeff and his brother were bought out of the company.

To this day, the company hasn't reached its full potential and has missed several waves within the industry when there could have been a great expansion and plenty for everyone. Unfortunately, when we become shortsighted and fearful, we can squeeze the life out of a business. When we treat employees unfairly rather than help them reach their full potential, we create ripple effects in our business that take away from true success. I believe this is what happened to this family business: Everyone was blinded, just like when Isaac mistook Jacob for Esau. The situation became very complex with many hidden agendas; most of all, the light within each other was disrespected. Each person lost their true connection to the Divine and acted out from that disconnection.

Jeff's choices at an early age set into action consequences that would dominate much of his adult life. It is hard to consider that each choice we make has such a ripple effect in creating probable future events. Sometimes we are blinded to the effects of our choices, especially if we act impulsively without considering God first, and without creating Sabbath moments that will enable us to consider the positive and negative consequences. Yet the end result happens when we take responsibility for the play of events that were set into action, reclaim our light and love for God within us, and move forward with new hope. We learn and grow from our choices as long as we take responsibility, relinquish blame and resentments, forgive ourselves and others, and finally move forward.

Even though the above situation seemed untenable, Jeff was also blessed with a wonderful son, Matthew David, whom he received custody of at the time of his divorce. When we embrace the whole picture of our lives with love and acceptance, we develop a deep sense of respect for our lives, release the negative love bonds, and embrace the positive ones. We never truly know the depth of our soul growth issues or God's plan for our life.

In the Jewish tradition, you are born into the Bible; the scripture you read on your 13th birthday represents your soul's journey. Years later, we found out that Jeff's Bar Mitzvah Torah Portion, to be memorized and spoken at his service, is Leviticus 16—the story of the scapegoat. Was this his life lesson, to learn how to master and release the negative love bonds in his family, to take on the negative projections so the family could heal? In the Scripture passage, Jeff could have taken the position of the goat, the priest, or the congregation who gathered together to confess and receive forgiveness for sins.

We were also surprised to find out that Jeff's Haftorah portion, a short selection from the Prophets read on every Sabbath that follows reading from the Torah, indicated that anyone who married outside of his tradition would suffer the consequences. Isn't it interesting that, according to Jewish tradition, Jeff was born into these life lessons! Are all of us born into Scripture, continuing to learn the life lessons of our ancestors?

A Battle of Will

In my family, the will of my maternal great-great-great grandfather, Edward West Sr., affected many generations because he sought to keep his money within the family bloodline. His oldest daughter, my Great-Great Grandmother Louise, had four children. Both her sister and brother were barren. After the premature death of both sisters in 1923 and 1925 respectively, my great-great-great grandfather chose to take care of all of his descendants for four generations in a way that caused a rift with his son. He included a clause in his written will that prevented any non-related adopted children from inheriting, so that any adoptive children Edward West Jr. might have would get nothing.

My great-great-great grandfather was astute and cared for his only son very much. He wanted him and his wife Dorothy to live off the dividends until his death, and then the dividends would be split between his wife and the other descendants. Each tier was paid out upon death except Dorothy's, whose portion would be redistributed among the remaining living heirs. But Edward West Jr. was upset that my mother's and her brother's descendants were to receive the final disbursement. This would cause a rift between family members, resulting in several years of isolation and scapegoating behavior toward my mother and her brother. Edward West Jr. plotted with other family members to fight my mother and her brother for their share in court. They were coveting my mother's and uncle's shares and felt it was their duty to take as much as possible, and create fraud.

My mother shared bits and pieces of stories about the will, but it wasn't until after her death, when I had to handle this part of her estate that I had in possession an actual copy of the will. After reading it a few times, I was as confused as ever, but I began to hear a voice that said, "Go back, Donna, and read it again. You don't understand yet what it means." So I went back over it again and again until I heard a story about each one of the people involved. It was as if my great-great-great grandfather and great-great grandmother were speaking to me. I would have to go to court to settle the estate with other family members whom I had never met. All of those who had already been paid out at the time of their parents' deaths came out to claim the remaining amount. They wanted the will to be settled by the courts so they would receive a major portion of the monies. All they needed to do was start contesting it. The coveting and entitlement still went on because they believed the stories they had been told. I often wondered why my mother's relatives never looked for us once my father took us away in 1958, and it all made perfect sense now. I was encouraged to stay strong and serendipitously hired one of the best estate lawyers, who knew all of the players, including the bank. We were able to negotiate an equitable settlement and heal this decades-old rift that had been based in coveting. If you'd like to see more details of this episode in my family history, you can review the genogram in Chapter 3.

This is why doing the genogram is so important. If you're not aware of it, you may be acting out something that is out of your control. In some of these cases, you can see two or three generations of this pattern being acted out. I hear inheritance stories all the time. Sometimes it works out beautifully, especially when parents talk beforehand to the whole family about what each child is to receive. There are healthy ways to do it while keeping the family in a unified place.

When it works out, the non-monetary payoff can be wondrous. I remember my father-in-law who, for several years, had wanted to cut his daughter out of his written will. Both my husband and I talked him out of it by showing him all the negative connotations that would go along with such a decision. I also helped him talk through the feelings that made him want to disinherit her in the first place. When he finally realized he didn't want to disinherit her after all and felt good about including her, his heart was lifted, as if he had healed something inside of himself. Last year, he went with his son Jeff and his wife Arlene to the bank to distribute some of his money before moving into an assisted living facility, due to his ailing health. While filling out the checks at the bank, he had a stroke and was rushed to the hospital. He told Jeff to go ahead and send off the check to his daughter. The next day, he passed away. When my sister-in-law heard that one of his last acts had been to write the inheritance check out to her, she burst into tears. Years of healing took place at long last.

How Can You Work Toward Healing?

If you want this same kind of healing for your family, you can begin by meditating on this Commandment and identifying any coveting issues you may have, including unfulfilled longings. Then consider the following and write the answers in your journal:

Tenth Commandment Reflections

Part 1

1. Can we learn anything from Cain's story today? What are your thoughts?
2. How do disapproval, rejection, and feelings of abandonment from God, parents, and educators cause such hostility in a person that it may lead to destructive behavior, even killing? Can you think of any examples?
3. How do you master your feelings of resentment, rage, and jealousy? Do you turn to God for love, understanding, and healing? What do you do?
4. What situations in your own life can you recall that resemble the Cain and Abel story?

Part 2

1. Do you covet another's blessings or successes?
2. How do you block your communication with God and your own blessings?
3. Where are you open to the blessings in your life?
4. How do you respect or disrespect God's direction for your life?
5. Contemplate and practice listening for God's direction. Pray without ceasing throughout the day for guidance in receiving blessings into your life.
6. Do you slow down to observe and contemplate your own behavior and moment toward success? If so, how? If not, what is blocking you?

7. Are you focusing on your own creativity and bringing forth your gifts and talents? If so, acknowledge the steps you have taken. If your answer is no, why not? What steps do you need to take?
8. Do you honor and respect God by giving back your first fruits, the best of your labor? If so, How? If not, what can you do now?
9. What do you need to change in yourself to connect with God within and work toward reaching your Divine potential?

Part 3

1. Is there anywhere in your life where you would like to be successful and are not currently experiencing success?
2. List areas of unhappiness. Meditate on each area.
3. How do you block your own success and or happiness?
4. Have you listened for God's direction and insights into these areas?
5. What can you change or do differently?

Part 4

1. Do you have an inheritance story to tell? Try to think through all the aspects and their effects on each person. Did it turn out well? Why? If not, why not?
2. If you haven't considered inheritance in your family lineage over the past four generations, consider looking into the gifts or issues around money. Do some of these unspoken positions affect you or others in your family? How?

On a positive note, we may want to contemplate how coveting another's possession has inspired us to work toward our own potential. Can you think of inspiring people in your life, someone you have wanted to emulate? This is coveting, too, albeit in a good way. You are not giving your power away but choosing a good role model to follow. You may ask, "How did they become so successful? What kind of time and energy did they put into their success? What is their attitude, and do they actually affect the universal mind of God with positive healthy desires? Do they face challenges and failure with an upbeat attitude and try again?" We do learn by watching others and following in their footsteps. We just need to watch our own footing and wear our own shoes on the path. In this way, we are inspired to fulfill our potential rather than taking on another's path. We are inspired to become the best we can be in the world and contribute to the betterment of society.

God actually wants us to use the creative life force within us to create anything we want. By understanding this Key, you unlock the doorway to your hidden potential. You will access the Divine substance within you and bring your own ideas and desires into manifestation. Without understanding this Key, you may always dream about another's success, life, or belongings without knowing how to achieve the same for yourself. God lets us know that we can access the same creative life force by staying in tune and trusting that all things manifest from the one Creator. You and I have the same power to access the Divine, so why not try today? Affirm your life and activate this creative force inside of you. Uncover your true dreams and desires and allow yourself to speak these into the mind of God. The power of your spoken word actually activates the universal consciousness in your favor. What do you need to do next? Take the steps to reach your full potential!

Reflections on the Ten Keys

Now that you have explored each of the Ten Spiritual Keys and discovered the secret—opening your heart, soul, eyes, and hands to emanate the Divine from within you—the opportunity to share your light with your partner, your family, and the world naturally follows. You have awakened the Divine potential within you to heal your family's generational negative love bonds and to return to living a God-Realized life. You deserve the Keys to self-mastery and restoration of your Divine birthright. Your family will be held within the light of Divine grace and love when you work with each Key. Remember, you may hit some bumps in the road, encountering old patterns that strive to hold you hostage to the past, but you can still claim the light within by placing each Key in your heart, soul, eyes, and hands. I encourage you to explore how you are feeling now and take an inventory of your experience.

1. What are your thoughts about the Ten Spiritual Keys? Do you believe or follow them? Have you contemplated them in conjunction with your relationship with God? Explain more.
2. Which Commandment (Key) do you find most difficult to follow? Were any of the Commandments broken by your family or ancestors? How did breaking the Commandments affect your family? Who was affected most? What happened?
3. Who taught you the Ten Commandments? Did they understand their true meaning and follow them?
4. Have you taught the Keys to your children? If so, why? If not, why?
5. Meditate on teaching the Keys to your children. What are the benefits?
6. If you have broken a Commandment or Key, how has that been passed onto your children or other significant people in your life? Are your children or significant others affected by your disconnection from God and the Commandments?
7. Can you trace a problem you see in the world as it relates to one or more of God's Commandments being broken? Refer to Chapters 3 and 4.

Once you have explored the Keys and created your own God-Realization Genogram, you will have a map to self-mastery. Moses was given these Keys to restore his people and bring them out of bondage. You, too, can come out of bondage and fulfill your Divine potential by working with each Key. Give the process a try! It's simple, and you will find it freeing!

PART 3

NEXT STEPS

Chapter 15

Restoring Your Divine Qualities

May today be peace within. May you trust your highest power that you are exactly where you are meant to be... May you not forget the infinite possibilities that are born of faith. May you use those gifts that you have received, and pass on the love that has been given to you... May you be content knowing you are a child of God... Let this presence settle into your bones, and allow your soul the freedom to sing, dance, praise, and love. It is there for each and every one of you. Mother Teresa

So here we are! At this point, we have traveled across many varied landscapes in your spiritual journey. We have covered all of the Ten Commandments, and you are ready to work on exploring your family tree, unearthing broken or weak limbs, and looking for places, people, or situations that require healing. You're probably all fired up: At last you have something you can do and you know what it is. You're in the car, the keys are in the ignition, and you're pulling out of the driveway. But let me ask you this: Where are you going? Will you recognize your destination when you arrive? Don't worry! I often see clients get so busy doing a genogram and so wrapped up in the stories of their ancestors' pasts that they forget to think about what they want to accomplish. Keep your eye on the road ahead!

I invite you to think about what you want for yourself and your family. What does it look like? Some of us might say we want to "be happy," but what does that really mean? Some of us might want our family to "feel better," but what does that mean? I'd like to challenge you to go deeper, to think about something more specific than happiness. Think about the core of who you are and the light that resides within you. How can you claim your spiritual roots and explore your Divine destiny?

If there are broken Spiritual Keys in your family, this pain will cover over certain essential elements of who you are. If you feel bad and yearn to be happy or feel better, then aspects of you that contribute greatly to your health and well-being have been suppressed. I call these aspects your Divine qualities, and have adapted them from my work with Dr. Barbara Brennan. Our very existence rests or resides within seven Divine qualities, seedpods of Divinity. These Divine qualities act as potential expressions of our Divine nature. They are fundamental to our existence and build the foundation for healthy physical, emotional, mental, interpersonal, and spiritual well-being. A breach (such as one that may be uncovered in a God-Realization Genogram) will cause a void that suppresses or obscures one or more of the Divine qualities within you or your family.

If these fundamental qualities are not mirrored through our primary relationships at birth, they will lie dormant as hidden potential. We can develop both positive and negative traits in response to our experiences with ancestors, parents, peers, educators, and community. Yet, if we return to these seven primary Divine qualities we will find the foundations for a healthy family life stored within us. So, the goal of this work—your destination once you're in the car—is to restore these qualities within.

Notices that I've use the word restore. I want you to understand that these qualities are already present in you; indeed, they are innate in every person. They come from the ray of light within us and they shine, unless they are covered by issues such as coveting or adultery. As we've already shared, God has given us the Ten Commandments as a way to master our negative impulses and dissolve whatever may cover our light. This process allows the rays of light from our Divine qualities to shine out fully from within us. Let's explore the following qualities next:

Divine Trust
Divine Self-Love and Self Acceptance
Divine Respect
Divine Interpersonal love
Divine Communication
Divine Vision
Divine Wisdom

The Divine Quality of Trust

This quality depends on our trust in God, which supports trust in ourselves and allows us to build trusting relationships with others. Removing the barriers that block our relationship with God restores our ability to trust in ourselves; it removes self-doubt and allows us to build relationships based in God's grace and love. Trust arises from deep within us and supports the healthy development of our minds, bodies, and spirits, especially our hearts and limbic systems, which are directly connected to bonding.

For some of us, finding trust in God will require that we unravel our misconceptions and mistrust in God. We must acknowledge the mistrust we have—not just in God, but also in ourselves and in others. Only then can we hope to open up to new awareness. We will not be able to "pour new wine into an old wineskin." When our perceptions change toward knowing the God within us, we form a new wine skin that dissolves betrayals, wounds, hurts, and restores us to wholeness.

Sometimes it is easier to uncover our mistrust in others, especially if we have been betrayed or hurt. We can also uncover our own shortcomings, such as when we have betrayed ourselves and made wrong decisions that compromised our integrity or self-care. Whatever the case, honestly facing our mistrust in God can be the key that unlocks the doorway to finding God's grace and love within us, and to restoring our trust. Working at these three levels—trusting in God, trusting in self, and trusting in others—can bring balance into our lives. If we place more trust in ourselves or someone else than in God and then fail, we can be riddled with pain, self-judgments, blame, and shame. Our inability to place God first can cause a tremendous amount of upheaval, as it does not allow any room for forgiveness for our shortcomings or of other people's faults. Placing God first does not guarantee there will be no pain. But it will open us to a different level of experience, to being held by God's grace, love, and mercy so that we can more clearly see the way home.

The Divine Quality of Self-love and Self-Acceptance

When we trust deeply in God and the unconditional love within us, the Divine quality of self-love and self-acceptance can emerge. Our Creator's omnipotent love for us is the sustenance of self-love and self-acceptance. These days, we can really make a mess of love and lose track of what it means. But this quality is so important and essential that it is the basis of the first story in the Bible.

Early on in the Scriptures, we are told to master our impulses and listen to God's direction for our lives. Still, even when we follow our own impulses, lose our connection with God, and suffer the consequences; we are unconditionally, eternally loved—despite our actions. Both Adam and Eve were loved by God, even after their choice to eat from the Tree of Knowledge. As a consequence of their disobedience, they lost their awareness of their omnipotent oneness with God. However, God continued to love and guide them and their descendants—all of us—in ways to restore our relationship with God. Eventually, He even sent His son to die on our behalf. God's love is so vast that it permeates the universe, and our capacity to experience this love—in all its forms—is the greatest gift residing within us. Divine self-love and self-acceptance is essential to our physiological, psychological, and spiritual development.

Opening to our Creator's love, compassion, and forgiveness teach us how to forgive ourselves. When we focus on loving God, it allows us to heal areas where we have criticized or judged ourselves harshly. In fact, Christ teaches that to truly love others, you need to start from an inner place of humble self-love and self-acceptance. Then we can love and accept others, forgiving them for their trespasses and praying for their restoration. Such compassion sustains us and nourishes our hearts and deep limbic systems.

We first experience this Divine quality as children, in our parents' ability to reflect unconditional love and acceptance to us. Through their love and acceptance, we learn to love and accept ourselves and others, regardless of our flaws. The good news is that even if parents don't reflect love, we still have the ability to experience and express unconditional love and acceptance, arising from our innate Divine nature. We must simply take the next step of calling forth this quality by creating a relationship with our Source, the Divine within.

The Divine Quality of Respect

We all want to be respected, and we have a finely tuned sense of when someone is disrespecting us. But where does that sense come from? What exactly does it take for us to respect others? Again, as with the other Divine qualities, the tendency to respect is already present. It emerges when we respect the Divine within us, as well as through our deep trust in God. Learning that God resides deep within and loves us unconditionally builds our authentic self-esteem and integrity. Our true identity emerges from this knowledge and supports our ability to honor and respect our relationships. Understanding this concept relinquishes self-doubt and fosters our intuitive wisdom; we recognize that God is within all sentient life.

The difficulty, of course, is in remembering all this and acting accordingly. That's where the Ten Commandments come in. As we have already learned, God gave us these highly effective ways—these Ten Spiritual Keys—to reflect on how we disrespect the Divine within us. As you have learned, the Keys open our hearts, souls, eyes, and hands to the light within, so you can master your impulses when confronted with various challenges. The Keys are the foundation to your own moral code; they make up your conscience and attune you to communicate directly with God. God has tried to teach all of our ancestors about the Divine quality of respect, from Adam and Eve to Cain and Abel to Abram and Sarai, through Moses, the prophets, and Christ—right down to us, where we are today. These Spiritual Keys restore our relationship with the Divine within us and heal our shortcomings. They bring us back once more to recognize God's presence in ourselves and in our relationships. Respect blossoms in this awareness, and it is essential to our health and well-being.

The Divine Quality of Interpersonal Love

This quality is built on the foundations of trust, self-love and self-acceptance, and respect for God. In order to open our hearts and unconditionally give and receive love with others, each of the first three Divine qualities must be developed or restored. When we are rooted in trust, self-love and self-acceptance, and respect, our hearts can fully open to reflect unconditional love to others. These three qualities directly affect our ability to bond with others and create positive love bonds. When these qualities are suppressed and undeveloped, we form negative love bonds with others. For example, when trust, love, acceptance and respect are provided an infant or child feels secure, loved, and part of the whole. When these qualities are lacking infants or children bond their love with anxiety, mistrust, rejection, and a sense of not belonging to the whole. The deep limbic system pairs love either with the positive experience or with the negative experience.

We can explore the New Testament to learn how Christ reunites us with God's boundless love and grace within us. Then we come to understand the importance of loving others as we humbly love ourselves. Our work is to become more like Christ in our relationships: to learn forgiveness, to clear the negative love bonds, and to restore the Divine within so we can build healthy, loving interpersonal relationships.

The Divine Quality of Communication

When we have fully developed the previous Divine qualities, we open an essential pathway—the pathway of communication. Trust, love and acceptance, respect, and interpersonal love all support our ability to listen for deeper wisdom and speak to others from this wisdom. When we can hear the deeper wisdom in conversations and respond from the light within us, healthy relatedness naturally follows. Opening ourselves to Divine communication allows us to take in nourishment from others while dissolving any conflicts or harshness from the outside world. We are able to discern the truth and communicate with others from the Divine within us.

Developing the previous qualities is so necessary that we can track our miscommunication by reflecting on them. Whenever we are out of balance in our ability to hear or speak the truth, we can find an underlying cause emerging from mistrust, self-judgment, loss of our respect or self-esteem, and judgments or resentments of others. Again, in the Bible the first lesson of human struggle focuses on communication. In the stories of Adam and Eve, Cain and Abel, Abram and Sarai, we learn how challenging it is to listen to and follow God's direction. We are told of their ability to hear God's instructions directly and indirectly through dreams or angels, yet each of them still struggles with following the insights or instructions so clearly spoken to them.

Learning to listen to God within enhances our understanding of our inner world and our communication with others. In return, we are able to hear about unfavorable aspects of ourselves and others in a non-defensive way. Our brains are able to relax, and not remaining in a heightened state of fight or flight, they can support effective communication and positive love bonds. When we reflect and refocus our attention on the underlying quality that needs to be restored, our communication with God, ourselves, and others grows clearer.

The Divine Quality of Vision

The quality of vision refers to our ability to open our eyes and see the truth from the Divine within. Each of the previous qualities brings clarity to our eyes and grants us the ability to see beyond our limited perceptions. Our vision becomes universally oriented and brings higher clarity to our relationships, business, and community service.

When our eyes and visual perceptions are based on trusting in God, authentic self-love and self-acceptance, respect, interpersonal love, and open communication, we are capable of creating unity and peace on Earth. When we surrender our distortions and see the world from God's perspective, we open ourselves to a myriad of possibilities. Our cone of perception widens, we understand the underlying causes of separation, and we see the underlying beauty in all of humanity and the world in which we live. Our eyes become focused on the Divine within all life.

The Divine Quality of Wisdom

This seventh Divine quality brings higher wisdom to each situation and opens us beyond thought to know God within. We know truth and have insights that we can trust beyond our linear rational mind. We are connected to the Universal Consciousness, from which all ideas arise. Our greater wisdom and solutions come from this knowing, which opens by transmitting all of the previous qualities. You are in tune with your inner light as it is expressed throughout your whole being. By focusing on God and allowing each of these Divine qualities to emerge, you clear your mind to directly know higher wisdom and truth. Each of the previous qualities clears any imbalance to allow for Divine wisdom to permeate your consciousness. The radiance of your mind, body, and spirit become one with the mind of God. Your consciousness expresses itself from a place of universal knowing. Seeing the higher truth of a situation allows you to express unity and peace.

God's radiant grace is forever an intricate aspect of your consciousness and wisdom. It really helps to know and remember this, because it is the key to resolving your problems and creating universal peace and harmony. Aligning all of ourselves with God's radiant grace prepares our consciousness to give a wonderful gift to our children and descendants for a thousand generations. There could be no greater love to give to our families, friends, communities, and country than to be faithful to God, to keep His Commandments, and to know His radiant grace.

Born into the Divine Qualities

Now imagine yourself being born into the Divine qualities. Your parents, your ancestors, and other relatives have all radiated Divine consciousness at the time of your birth. Each one of these qualities mirrors your Divine nature, the light within you. In Part 1, you learned that you are born into your Family Tree of Knowledge. Now it is time to consider what it looks like when your consciousness is unencumbered by the generational negative love bonds. Imagine each quality as a state of consciousness that nourishes your physical, psychological, interpersonal, and spiritual development. Working all together they inspire you to reach your divine potential in any given moment. The qualities of the Divine are interdependent and create a health matrix of Divine consciousness like a holographic image of interdependence, and something like the chart below.

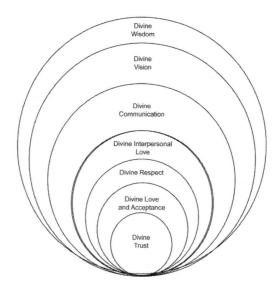

Born into Unexpressed Divine Qualities

Since we are also born into these concentric circles of our families' generational struggles and negative love bonds, it is important to visualize how we are affected by the Divine light being blocked—like being born under the bushel of generational negative love bonds. These unresolved issues block us from reaching our Divine potential. And remember, each of us may be blocked in one or more areas.

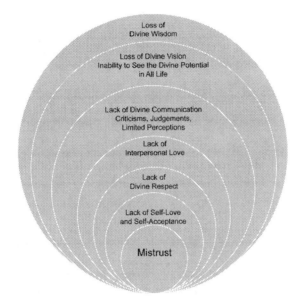

But when it comes to blocked Divine qualities, remember that God has given us a way to transform our heartache, pain, and generational negative love bonds: the Ten Spiritual Keys. The Keys open us to our Divine potential to heal and restore the light within us. When you meditate on them, you open your heart, soul, eyes, and hands to the Divine light within and begin to live from a point of Divine grace.

Imagine what it has been like to be born into both your maternal and paternal family heritage. There is so much to embrace and uncover so your light can shine forth, so you can bring this light to your partner and family. You may be excited to begin this journey and want more support and tools, especially when you hit a bump in the road.

Another way you can restore the qualities is to use the *I AM* Meditation. I give a brief explanation of the meditation here, and you can explore it in more depth by reading my forthcoming book, *Restoring Our Divine Nature: The I AM Meditation Workbook*. This process along with the keys opens you to feeling the blessings from a thousand generations and to your reentry into the Garden of Eden. You will have the keys of self-mastery and well-being for yourself, your family, your work, and your community. For now, let's explore the *I AM* Meditation and how it can help you bring balance to your life.

The *I AM* Meditation

This meditation is another way to bring your mind, body, and spirit into harmony and peace. Along with meditating on the Ten Keys and working with your God-Realization Genogram, this tool can be used in self-healing. You can use it at work, driving in your car, and in walking meditations. And you don't have to be an expert in meditation to benefit from reciting these words. You can use it to bring balance to any of the negative love bonds, negative beliefs, or negative emotions you might experience, bringing peace and harmony to any situation. It works with your energy-consciousness system and your deep limbic system to restore peace and harmony.

The words of the meditation are as follows:

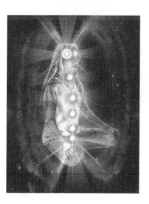

I Know Divine Wisdom from the *I AM that I AM*

I See Divine Truth from the *I AM that I AM*

I Communicate Divine Truth from the *I AM that I AM*

I Relate to Others from the *I AM that I AM*

I Respect the *I AM that I AM*

I Love and Accept the *I AM that I AM*

I Trust in the *I AM that I AM*

In doing the *I AM* Meditation, you'll discover that its power comes from the divine within you—from your voice expressing consistent affirmation. You will feel your energy rising to meet the vibration rate of the words as you chant them. With this new energy, you'll be able to heal pain and remove defensive blocks arising from negative thinking and overdramatized emotions. For some people, this may be difficult, especially if your earliest childhood memories are based on mistrust, stemming from neglect or abuse. But through the power of your own spoken words, these mantras have the ability to transform the old beliefs that are holding you hostage to recycled patterns or painful memories. You'll be able to release these old internalized tapes that are based in fear, mistrust, and negative thinking and replace them with a healthy sense of trust.

To learn more about how to work with the seven Divine qualities and the *I AM* Meditation, you can visit my website (www.livingfromgrace.com), order *Restoring Our Divine Nature: The* I AM *Meditation Workbook,* or sign up for a live workshop.

The Path

I invite you to bring together these tools—the God-Realization Genogram, the Ten Commandments, the seven Divine qualities, and the *I AM* Meditations. As you're working on your family issues, pray on your Family Tree of Knowledge, awaken and restore your connection in your heart, in your soul, and in your hands. What are your experiences? Can you awaken from within, resolve a wound, and release the negative love bond? Letting go of a negative love bond causes a deep limbic shift and change. It's sort of like an album skipping on an old phonograph. You might be across the room listening to the skipping and wishing the needle would move forward, but the situation will not resolve itself. You must finally get up and move the needle over one ridge so it plays the rest of the song. When something in the limbic system plays over and over again in a negative pattern, we need to move it one ridge over to play the Divine quality instead.

It takes some focus to make this shift, but it is possible. We are meant to communicate with God and to master our own energy and impulses; when those seven Divine qualities and our tools of self-mastery are in play, we can become the living light. We can transcend any problems in our lives, we can heal our generational negative love bonds, and we can claim the blessings of a thousand generations. In this process, you can expect higher levels of Divinity to come through you. The difference between being self-realized and God-realized is moving into this higher level of light shining through you.

Learning how to identify negative love bonds and restore our original Divine qualities will provide the basis for living a healthy, fruitful life. By unraveling the crooked paths that hold us hostage to negative cycles, and by releasing the blame, shame, and guilt, we become free to live from Divine grace and love. We can still choose to focus on all the wrongs of our ancestors, but doing so keeps us from raising our vibration to a higher level of understanding. It's an ongoing process. Whenever we get caught up with what's been holding us back, thinking this is our lot in life entraps us in the hypnotic stupor of those issues rather than expanding beyond them.

We must connect to our light and help transform any instances when, in the past few generations, people have fallen from grace and lost their spiritual connections to the Divine light within them. That's the whole spiritual journey: to get back to the Garden of Eden, to unravel those greater mysteries and those hidden crooked paths so we can all be born into the light again. We can reclaim every Divine quality given to us and offer them in our relationships with our spouses, children, and communities. Each person has the potential to experience the light within us, to receive the blessings of our ancestral heritage, and to know the blessings of the Divine, regardless of religious orientation. When we relate with each other from this place, we can see that others are also blessed. Embodying and living the God-Realization process offers peace with others and true peace on Earth.

Remember this: You also had ancestors who did right, those who walked in the light of their own pure Divinity. Their light is continuously being transmitted to you and to all your family. They are reaching out to you now with the blessings of a thousand generations. I invite you to embrace your heritage and birthright, but know the journey will not be an easy one. You will find obstacles at every turn, but ultimately, the healing experienced by you and your family will be worth the exploration. And with God, of course, all things are possible. Let the restoration begin!

BIBLIOGRAPHY

Albright, Rausch, Carol, and Ashbrook B. James. *Where God Lives in the Human Brain.* (Sourcebooks, April 2001, ISBN 1570717419).

Atwood & Schwartz. Extramarital Sex Statistics. In *Journal of Couple & Relationship Therapy,* 2002. (http://www.menstuff.org/issues/byissue/infidelitystats.html)

Amen MD, Daniel G. *Change Your Brain, Change Your Life: The Breakthrough Program for Conquering Anxiety, Depression, Obsessiveness, Anger and Impulsiveness.* (Three Rivers Press, December 1999, ISBN 0812929985).

Brennan, Barbara Ann. *Hands of Light: A Guide to Healing Through the Human Energy Field.* (Bantam, May 1988, ISBN 0553345397).

Brennan, Barbara Ann. *Light Emerging: The Journey of Personal Healing.* (Bantam, November 1993, ISBN 0553354566).

Discovery Channel School, Great Books: Dante's Inferno Video. (Discover Communications Inc., Bethesda, MD 20814-3579, 2003, ISBN 1-58738-419-1).

Engelbrite(Stone), Michael Peter (Stone). *American King James Version.* (Completed Version published for public domain November 8, 1999.)

Gladwell, Malcolm. *Outliers: The Story of Success.* (Little Brown & Co., November 2008, ISBN 0316017922).

God's Word, New International Version: Containing the Old and New Testament (NIV). (International Bible Society, 1973,1978, 1984, ASIN B000X9TVXA).

Jablonka, Eva and Lamb, Marion. *Epigenetic Inheritance and Evolution: The Lamarckian Dimension.* (Oxford University Press, May 1995, ISBN 0198540639).

Jones, Alexander. *The Jerusalem Bible: Readers Edition* (Doubleday Religion, February 2000, ISBN 0385499183).

Lipton, Bruce H. *The Biology of Belief: Unleashing the Power of Consciousness, Matter, and Miracles.* (Hay House, September 2008, ISBN 1401923119).

The Mitzvah Torah: The Five Books of Moses: A New Translation of the Holy Scriptures According to the Masoretic Text. (The Jewish Publication Society, 1962, 1992).

Meyers, Joyce (Notes and Commentary).*The Everyday Life Bible: The Amplified Version.* (Faith Words, Hachette Book Group USA, ISBN-13: 978-0-446-57826-4, ISBN_10: 0-446-57826-6)

Newberg, Andrew MD, and Waldman, Robert Mark. *How God Changes Your Brain: Breakthrough Findings of a Neuroscientist.* (Ballantine Books, March 2010, ISBN 0345503422, pp. 16,114).

Newberg, Andrew MD, and Waldman, Robert Mark. *Born To Believe: God, Science, and the Origin of Ordinary and Extraordinary Beliefs.* (Free Press, October 2007, ISBN 0743274989).

Pert, Candace. *Molecules of Emotion: The Science Behind Mind-Body Medicine.* (Simon & Schuster, February 1999, ISBN 0684846349).

Ruggiero,David A., PhD. *Thalamocortical, Reticular, and Limbic Systems.* (http://neuroscienceupdate.cumc.columbia.edu/popups/pdfs/DavidRuggiero.pdf)

Strauss Evans, Donna. *Blessings From a Thousand Generations: Companion Workbook.* Forthcoming in 2011. (www.livingfromgrace.com)

Strauss Evans, Donna. *Restoring Our Divine Nature: The* I AM *Meditation Workbook.* Forthcoming in 2011. (www.livingfromgrace.com)

Whitfield, MD. L. Charles. *The Truth about Mental Illness: Choice for Healing.* (Health Communications Inc., April 2004, ISBN 075730107X).

Other Resources

Strauss Evans, Donna. *I AM* Meditation (CD; www.livingfromgrace.com)

Genogram Symbol Chart. (http://en.wikipedia.org/wiki/Genogram#Genogram_symbols)

Great Quotes. (http://www.greatquotes.com)

Famous Quotes And Authors. (www.famousquotesandauthors.com)